Vincent van Gogh

1853–1890

Vincent van Gogh

For Art and for Life

Translated by Arnold Pomerans

PENGUIN ARCHIVE

PENGUIN BOOKS

UK | USA | Canada | Ireland | Australia
India | New Zealand | South Africa

Penguin Books is part of the Penguin Random House group of companies
whose addresses can be found at global.penguinrandomhouse.com.

Penguin Random House UK,
One Embassy Gardens, 8 Viaduct Gardens, London sw11 7bw

penguin.co.uk

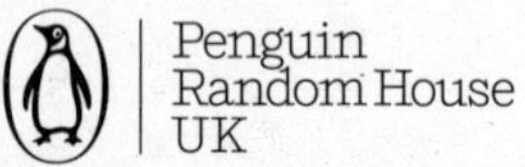

The Letters of Vincent van Gogh, selected and edited by Ronald de Leeuw,
first published by Allen Lane The Penguin Press 1996
This selection published in Penguin Classics 2025
005

Translation copyright © Sdu Publishers, 1997

No part of this book may be used or reproduced in any manner for the
purpose of training artificial intelligence technologies or systems. In accordance
with Article 4(3) of the DSM Directive 2019/790, Penguin Random House
expressly reserves this work from the text and data mining exception.

Set in 11.2/13.75pt Dante MT Std
Typeset by Jouve (UK), Milton Keynes
Printed and bound in Great Britain by Clays Ltd, Elcograf S.p.A.

The authorized representative in the EEA is Penguin Random House Ireland,
Morrison Chambers, 32 Nassau Street, Dublin D02 YH68

A CIP catalogue record for this book is available from the British Library

ISBN: 978–0–241–75246–3

Penguin Random House is committed to a sustainable future
for our business, our readers and our planet. This book is made from
Forest Stewardship Council® certified paper.

Contents

Biographical Outline

1853   Vincent Willem van Gogh born at Groot-
Zundert, Netherlands on 30 March

1857   Birth of his favourite brother, Theodorus
(Theo), on 1 May

1869   On 30 July, van Gogh joins the international
art dealers, Goupil & Cie, in The Hague

1873–5   Works for Goupil in London and Paris

1876   Dismissed from Goupil at the end of March;
he becomes a teacher in Ramsgate and an
assistant preacher in Isleworth

1877   Moves to Amsterdam in May to prepare
for the entrance examination to the
theological faculty

1878   In July he formally abandons his studies
in Theology and moves to the Borinage in
December to work as an evangelist among
the miners

1879   In July van Gogh decides to become an artist

1881   Moves into his parents' house in Etten

1882   In January he rents a studio in The Hague;
in March, he receives his first commission,
for twelve views of The Hague

1883	He moves into his parents' house in Neunen in December
1885	He moves to Antwerp in November and hopes to earn a living there with townscapes and portraits
1886	He leaves for Paris in March and moves in with Theo; he makes friends with Henri de Toulouse-Lautrec and others; he discovers the true meaning of Impressionism. In the summer, he paints a series of still lifes with flowers as colour studies
1888	On 19 February, exhausted by the pressures of life in Paris and driven by a great longing for rest and a warm climate, he leaves for Arles in the south of France. He invites Gauguin to live and work with him in the Yellow House; however, their conflicting views on art make working together increasingly difficult. Following a violent argument with Gauguin, he cuts off part of his ear on 23 December and Gauguin leaves precipitately for Paris; he is admitted to the hospital in Arles and treated by Dr Félix Rey
1889	Contrary to all expectations, he recovers quickly and returns to the Yellow House on 7 January. At the end of April he decides to become a voluntary patient

at Saint-Paul-de-Mausole, a psychiatric institution in nearby Saint-Rémy-de Provence. He has a sudden attack in mid-July while out painting in the fields and is unable to return to work until early September; at the end of December he has another attack, lasting one week

1890   On 18 January the seventh annual exhibition of the Vingtistes in Brussels, which includes six of his paintings, opens; at the end of January he has another attack lasting a week; on 25 January he receives Albert Aurier's laudatory article entitled 'Les Isolés: Vincent van Gogh'. He visits Arles on 22 February and has another attack, which lasts until the end of April. He arrives in Auvers on 20 May and is placed in the care of Dr Paul Gachet, a physician and amateur artist. He shoots himself in the chest on 27 July and dies of his wounds on 29 July in Theo's presence

1891   On 25 January Theo dies at the age of thirty-three

In this edition, the letters D and F in square brackets indicate whether a particular letter was originally written in Dutch or French. The numbering is standard across van Gogh literature.

I

Becoming an Artist

The Borinage

136 [F]

Cuesmes, 24 Sept. 1880

Dear Theo,

Your letter has done me good and I thank you for having written to me in the way you have.

The roll with a new selection of etchings & various prints has just arrived. First and foremost the masterly etching, Le buisson, by Daubigny / Ruysdael. Well! I propose to make two drawings, in sepia or something else, one after that etching, the other after Le four dans les Landes by Th. Rousseau. Indeed, I have already done a sepia of the latter, but if you compare it with Daubigny's etching you will see that it contrasts feebly, although considered on its own the sepia may betray some tone & sentiment. I shall have to return to it & tackle it again.

I am still working on Bargue's Cours de dessin & intend to finish it before I go on to anything else, for both my hand and my mind are growing daily more supple & strong as a result, & I cannot thank Mr Tersteeg enough for having been so kind as to lend it to me. The models are outstanding. Meanwhile I am reading one book on anatomy & another on perspective, which Mr Tersteeg also sent me. These studies are demanding & sometimes the books are extremely tedious, but I think all the same that it's doing me good to study them.

So you see that I am working away hard, though for the moment it is not yielding particularly gratifying results. But I have every hope that these thorns will bear white blooms in due course & that these apparently fruitless struggles are nothing but labour pains. First the pain, then the joy.

You mention Lessore. I think I remember some very elegant watercolour landscapes by him in a blond tone, worked with an apparent ease & a light touch, yet with accuracy & distinction, & a somewhat decorative effect (that is not meant badly, but on the contrary, in a favourable sense). So I know a little about his work & you mention someone not entirely unknown to me.

I admire the portrait of Victor Hugo. It is done very conscientiously with the evident intention of portraying the truth without straining after effect. That is precisely what makes it so effective.

Last winter I pored over some of Hugo's works, Le dernier jour d'un condamné & an excellent book on Shakespeare. I first started studying this writer long ago. He is just as splendid as Rembrandt. Shakespeare is to Charles Dickens or V. Hugo what Ruysdael is to Daubigny, & Rembrandt to Millet.

What you say in your letter about Barbizon is perfectly true & I can tell you one or two things that will make it clear how much I share your view. I haven't been to Barbizon, but though I haven't been there, I did go to Courrières last winter. I went on a walking tour in the Pas-de-Calais, not the English Channel but the department, or province. I had gone on this trip in the hope of perhaps finding some sort of work there, if possible – I would have accepted anything – but in fact I set out a bit reluctantly, though I can't say exactly why. But I had told myself, you must see Courrières. I had just 10 francs in my pocket and because I had started out by taking the train, that was soon gone, & as I was on the road for a week, it was a rather gruelling trip.

Anyway, I saw Courrières & the outside of M. Jules Breton's studio. The outside of the studio was a bit of a disappointment, seeing that it is a brand-new studio, recently built of brick, of a Methodist regularity, with an inhospitable, stone-cold & forbidding aspect, just like C. M.'s Jovinda, which, between ourselves, I am none too keen on either, for the same reason. If I could have seen the inside, I am quite certain that I should have given no further thought to the outside, but there you are, I could not see the inside because I dared not introduce myself and go in. Elsewhere in Courrières I looked for traces of Jules Breton or any other artist. All I was able to find was a portrait of him at a photographer's & a copy of Titian's Entombment in a corner of the old church which looked very beautiful to me in the darkness & masterly in tone. Was it by him? I don't know because I was unable to make out any signature.

But of any living artist, no trace, just a café called the Café des Beaux Arts, also of new, inhospitable, stone-cold, repulsive brick – the café was decorated with a kind of fresco or mural depicting episodes from the life of that illustrious knight, Don Quixote.

To tell the truth, the frescos seemed to me rather poor consolation and fairly mediocre at the time. I don't know who did them.

But anyway I did see the country around Courrières then, the haystacks, the brown farmland or the marled earth, almost coffee-coloured (with whitish spots where the marl shows through), which seems somewhat unusual to people like us who are used to a blackish soil. And the French sky looked to me much finer & brighter than the smoky & foggy sky of the Borinage. What's more, there were farms & barns that, God be praised, still retained their mossy thatched roofs. I also saw the flocks of crows made famous by the pictures of Daubigny & Millet. Not to mention, as I ought to have done in the first place, the characteristic & picturesque figures of all manner of workmen, diggers, woodcutters, a farmhand driving his wagon & a silhouette of a woman with a white cap. Even in Courrières there was still a coal mine or pit, I saw the day shift come up at nightfall, but there were no women workers in men's clothes as in the Borinage, just the miners looking tired & careworn, black with coal dust, dressed in ragged miners' clothes, one of them in an old army cape.

Although this trip nearly killed me & though I came back spent with fatigue, with crippled feet & in a more or less depressed state of mind, I do not regret it, because I saw some interesting things and the terrible ordeals of suffering are what teach you to look at things through different eyes.

I earned a few crusts here and there en route in exchange for a picture or a drawing or two I had in my bag. But when my ten francs ran out I tried to bivouac in the open the last 3 nights, once in an abandoned carriage which was completely white with hoarfrost the next morning, not the best accommodation, once in a pile of faggots, and once, & that was a slight improvement, in a haystack that had been opened up, where I succeeded in making myself a slightly more comfortable little hideaway, though the drizzle did not exactly add to my enjoyment.

Well, even in these depths of misery I felt my energy revive & said to myself, I shall get over it somehow, I shall set to work again with my pencil, which I had cast aside in my deep dejection, & I shall draw again, & ever since I have had the feeling that everything has changed for me, & now I am in my stride & my pencil has become slightly more willing & seems to be getting more so by the day. My over-long & over-intense misery had discouraged me so much that I was unable to do anything.

I saw something else during the trip – the weavers' villages.

The miners & the weavers still form a race somehow apart from other workers & artisans and I have much fellow-feeling for them & should consider myself fortunate if I could draw them one day, for then these as yet unknown, or virtually unknown, types would be brought out into the light of day.

The man from the depths, from the abyss, 'de profundis', that is the miner. The other with the faraway look, almost daydreaming, almost a sleepwalker, that is the weaver. I have been living among them now for nearly 2 years & have learned a little of their special character, in particular that of the miners. And increasingly I find something touching & even pathetic in these poor, humble workers, the lowest of the low in a manner of speaking, and the most despised, who, owing to a possibly widely held but quite baseless and inaccurate presumption, are usually considered a race of knaves & scoundrels. Knaves, drunkards & scoundrels may be found here, of course, just as elsewhere, but the real type is nothing at all like that.

You refer vaguely in your letter to my coming sooner or later to Paris or its environs, if it were possible & if I wanted to. It is of course my eager & fervent wish to go either to Paris or to Barbizon, or somewhere else, but how can I, when I do not earn a cent and when, though I work hard, it will still be some time before I reach the point at which I can give any thought to something like going to Paris. For honestly, to be able to work properly I need at least a hundred francs a month. You can certainly live on less, but then you really are hard up, much too hard up in fact!

Poverty stops the best minds in their tracks, the old Palizzi saying goes, which has some truth in it & is entirely true if you understand its real meaning and import. For the moment I do not see how it could be feasible, and the best thing is for me to stay here & work as hard as I can, & after all, it is cheaper to live here.

At the same time I must tell you that I cannot remain very much longer in the little room where I live now. It is very small indeed, and then there are the two beds as well, the children's & my own. And now that I am working on Bargue's fairly large sheets I cannot tell you how difficult it is. I don't want to upset these people's domestic arrangements. They have already told me that I couldn't have the other room in the house under any circumstances, not even if I paid more, for the woman needs it for her washing, which in a miner's house has to be done almost every day. In short, I should like to rent a small workman's cottage. It costs about 9 francs a month.

I cannot tell you (though fresh problems arise & will continue to arise every day), I cannot tell you how happy I am that I have taken up drawing again. I had been thinking about it for a long time, but always considered it impossible & beyond my abilities. But now, though I continue to be conscious of my failings & of my depressing dependence on a great many things, now I have recovered my peace of mind & my energy increases by the day.

As far as coming to Paris is concerned, it would be of particular advantage to me if we could manage to establish contact with some good & able artist, but to be quite blunt about it, it might only be a repetition on a large scale of my trip to Courrières, where I hoped to come across a living example of the species Artist and found none. For me the object is to learn to draw well, to gain control of my pencil, my charcoal or my brush. Once I have achieved that I shall be able to do good work almost anywhere and the Borinage is as picturesque as old Venice, as Arabia, as Brittany, Normandy, Picardy or Brie.

Should my work be no good, it will be my own fault. But in Barbizon, you most certainly have a better chance than elsewhere of meeting a good artist who would be as an angel sent by God, should such a happy meeting take place. I say this in all seriousness and without exaggeration. So if, sometime or other, you should see the means & the opportunity, please think of me. Meanwhile I'll stay here quietly in some small workman's cottage and work as hard as I can.

You mentioned Meryon again. What you say about him is quite true. I know his etchings slightly. If you want to see something curious, then place one of his meticulous & powerful sketches next to a print by Viollet-le-Duc or anyone else engaged in architecture. If you do, then you will see Meryon in his true light, thanks to the other etching which will serve, whether you like it or not, as a foil or contrast. Right, so what do you see? This. Even when he draws bricks, granite, iron bars or the railing of a bridge, Meryon puts into his etchings something of the human soul, moved by I know not what inner sorrow. I have seen V. Hugo's drawings of Gothic buildings. Well, though they lacked Meryon's powerful and masterly technique, they had something of the same sentiment. What sort of sentiment is that? It is akin to what Albrecht Dürer expressed in his Melancholia, and James Tissot and M. Maris (different though these two may be) in our own day. A discerning critic once rightly said of James Tissot,

'He is a troubled soul.' However this may be, there is something of the human soul in his work and that is why he is great, immense, infinite. But place Viollet-le-Duc alongside and he is stone, while the other, that is, Meryon, is Spirit.

Meryon is said to have had so much love that, just like Dickens's Sydney Carton, he loved even the stones of certain places. But in Millet, in Jules Breton, in Jozef Israels, the precious pearl, the human soul, is even more in evidence and better expressed, in a noble, worthier, & if you will allow me, more evangelical tone.

But to return to Meryon, in my view he also has a distant kinship with Jongkind & perhaps with Seymour Haden, since at times these two artists have been extremely good.

Just wait, and perhaps you'll see that I too am a workman. Though I cannot predict what I shall be able to do, I hope to make a few sketches with perhaps something human in them, but first I must do the Bargue drawings and other more or less difficult things. Narrow is the way & strait the gate & there are only a few who find it.

Thanking you for your kindness, especially for Le buisson, I shake your hand,

Vincent.

I have now taken your whole collection, but you will get it back later and in addition I've got some very fine things for your collection of wood engravings, which I hope you will continue, in the 2 volumes of the Musée Universal which I am keeping for you.

Etten

150 [D]

[c. September 1881]

My dear Theo,

Though it is only a short time since I wrote to you, I have something more to tell you now.

For there has been a change in my drawings, both in the way I set about them and in the result.

Also, as a consequence of some of the things Mauve told me, I have started to work with live models again. Luckily I have been able to get several people to sit here for me, including Piet Kaufman, the labourer.

Careful study and the constant & repeated copying of Bargue's Exercices au fusain have given me a better insight into figure-drawing. I have learned to measure and to see and to look for the broad outlines, so that, thank God, what seemed utterly impossible to me before is gradually becoming possible now. I have drawn a man with a spade, that is 'un bêcheur',* 5 times over in a variety of poses, a sower twice, and a girl with a broom twice. Then a woman in a white cap peeling potatoes & a shepherd leaning on his crook and finally an old, sick peasant sitting on a chair by the hearth with his head in his hands and his elbows on his knees.

* A digger

And it won't be left at that, of course. Once a few sheep have crossed the bridge, the whole flock follows.

Now I must draw diggers, sowers, men & women at the plough, without cease. Scrutinize & draw everything that is part of country life. Just as many others have done & are doing. I no longer stand as helpless before nature as I used to do.

I brought along some conté-crayon in wood (just like pencils) from The Hague and I work with them a great deal now.

I have also started to introduce the brush and the stump. With a little sepia or India ink, and now and then with a little colour.

What is quite certain is that the drawings I have been doing lately bear little resemblance to anything I have done before.

The size of the figures is about the same as that of an Exercice au fusain.

As for landscape, I don't see why it need suffer in any way as a result. On the contrary, it will gain. Enclosed are a few small sketches to give you an idea.

Of course I have to pay the people who pose. Not much, but because it happens every day it is one expense more until I manage to sell some drawings.

But since a figure is hardly ever a complete failure, I am sure that the outlay on the model will be recovered in full relatively soon.

For nowadays anyone who has learned to tackle a figure and hang on to it until it is safely down on paper can earn quite a bit. I need hardly tell you that I am merely sending you these sketches to give you some idea of the pose. I dashed them off today in no time at all and can see that there is a lot wrong with the proportions, more so anyway than in the actual drawings. I've had a nice letter from Rappard, who seems to be hard at work. He sent me some very good landscape sketches. I wish he would come back here again for a few days.

This is a field or rather a stubble, where they are ploughing & sowing. Have made a fairly large sketch of it with a gathering thunderstorm.

The other two sketches are poses of diggers. I hope to do several more of them.

The other sower has a basket. I am tremendously anxious to get a woman to pose with a seed basket, so as to find a little figure like the one I showed you in the spring and which you can see in the foreground of the first little sketch.

Well, as Mauve says, the works are in full swing.

If you like and are able to, please remember the Ingres paper, the colour of unbleached linen, the stronger kind if possible. In any case, write as soon as you can, and accept a handshake in my thoughts,

Ever yours,
Vincent

152 [D]

[12–15 October 1881]

My dear Theo,

I was very pleased to get your letter just now, and as I intended to write to you anyhow in the next day or so, I am replying right away.

I'm so glad you've sent the Ingres paper. I've still got some left, but not the right colour.

I was happy to hear what Mr Tersteeg said to you about my drawings, and certainly no less glad that you saw progress yourself in the sketches I sent you. If that is indeed so, I mean to work to such effect that neither you nor Mr T. will have any reason to take back your more favourable opinions. I shall do my very best not to let you down.

The artist always comes up against resistance from nature in the beginning, but if he really takes her seriously he will not be put off by that opposition, on the contrary, it is all the more incentive to win her over – at heart, nature and the honest draughtsman are as one. (Nature is most certainly 'intangible', yet one must come to grips with her and do so with a firm hand.) And having wrestled and struggled with nature for some time now, I find her more yielding and submissive, not that I have got there yet, no one is further from thinking that than I am, but things are beginning to come more easily.

The struggle with nature is sometimes a bit like what Shakespeare calls 'taming the shrew' (which means wearing down the opposition, bon gré et mal gré*). In many fields, but especially in drawing, I think that 'serrer de près vaut mieux que lâcher'†.

I have come to feel more and more that figure drawing is an especially good thing to do, and that indirectly it also has a good effect on landscape drawing. If one draws a pollard willow as if it were a living being, which after all is what it is, then the surroundings follow almost by themselves, provided only that one has focused all one's attention on that particular tree and not rested until there was some life in it.

Enclosed are a few small sketches. I'm doing quite a bit of work on the Leurs road these days. Working with watercolour & sepia now and then too, but that isn't coming off too well yet.

Mauve has gone to Drenthe. We've agreed that I'll go and see him there as soon as he writes, but perhaps he'll come and spend a day at Prinsenhage first.

I went to see the Fabritius in Rotterdam on my last trip, and I'm glad you had a chance to see that Mesdag draw, among other things. If the drawing by Mrs Mesdag you mention is of yellow roses on a mossy ground, then I saw it at the exhibition and it is indeed very beautiful and artistic.

What you say about De Bock is, I think, true in every

* Willy-nilly

† Persistence is better than surrender

respect. I take the same view of him, but could not have put it as well as you did in your letter. If he could and wanted to concentrate, he would certainly be a better artist than he is. I told him straight out, 'De Bock, if you and I were to apply ourselves to figure drawing for a year, then we would both end up quite different from what we are now, but if we do not apply ourselves and simply carry on without learning anything new, then we won't even stay as we are but will lose ground. If we don't draw figures, or trees as if they were figures, then we have no backbone, or rather one that's too weak. Could Millet & Corot, of whom we both think so much, draw figures, or couldn't they? I think those Masters tackled just about anything.' And he agreed with me about this, in part at least.

In fact, I think he's been working very hard on the Panorama, and even though he refuses to admit it, that too will have a generally favourable effect on him.

He told me a very funny thing about the Panorama, which made me feel very warmly towards him. You know the painter Destrée. He went up to De Bock with a very superior air, and said to him, with great disdain, of course, yet in an unctuous and insufferably patronizing way, 'De Bock, they asked me to paint that Panorama, too, but seeing it was lacking in any artistic worth I felt I simply had to refuse.'

To which De Bock retorted, 'Mr Destrée, which is easier, painting a panorama or refusing to paint one? Which is more artistic, doing it or not doing it?' I'm not sure if those were his precise words, but that was certainly the gist of it, and I thought it straight to the point.

And I respect it as much as I respect your way of dealing with the older and wiser members of your society, whom you have left to their own old age and wisdom while you yourself have got on with things in your younger and more energetic way. That is true philosophy and makes us act as De Bock & you do when the need arises; it can be said of such philosophy that it is practical as well, in the same way as Mauve says, 'Painting is drawing as well.'

I've filled up my paper, so I shall end and go out for a walk. My warmest thanks for all your efforts on my behalf, a handshake in my thoughts, and believe me,

Ever yours,
Vincent

The Hague

218 [D]

[21 July 1882]

Dear brother,

It is already late, but I felt like writing to you again anyway. You are not here – but I need you & sometimes feel we are not far away from each other.

Today I promised myself something, that is, to treat my indisposition, or rather what remains of it, as if it didn't exist. Enough time has been lost, work must go on. So, well or not well, I am going back to drawing regularly from morning till night. I don't want anybody to be able to say to me again, 'Oh, but those are only old drawings.'

I drew a study today of the child's little cradle with some touches of colour in it. I am also at work on one like those meadows I sent you recently.

My hands have become a little too white for my liking, but that's too bad. I'm going to go back outdoors again, a possible relapse matters less to me than staying away from work any longer.

Art is jealous, she doesn't like taking second place to an indisposition. Hence I shall humour her. So you will, I hope, be receiving a few more reasonably acceptable things shortly.

People like me really <u>should</u> not be ill. I would like to make it perfectly clear to you how I look at art. To get to the essence of things one has to work long & hard.

What I want & have as my aim is infernally difficult to achieve, and yet I don't think I am raising my sights too high. I want to do drawings that will <u>touch</u> some people.

Sorrow is a small beginning – perhaps such little landscapes as the Meerdervoort Avenue, the Rijswijk Meadows, and the Dab Drying Shed are also a small beginning. There is at least something straight from my own heart in them. What I want to express, in both figure and landscape, isn't anything sentimental or melancholy, but deep anguish. In short, I want to get to the point where people say of my work: that man feels deeply, that man feels keenly. In spite of my so-called coarseness – do you understand? – perhaps for that very reason. It seems pretentious to talk like that now, but that is the reason why I want to put all my energies into it.

What am I in the eyes of most people – a nonentity, an eccentric, or an unpleasant person – somebody who has no position in society and never will have, in short, the lowest of the low.

All right, then – even if that were absolutely true, then I should one day like to show by my work what such an eccentric, such a nobody, has in his heart.

That is my ambition, based less on resentment than on love malgré tout,[*] based more on a feeling of serenity than on passion.

Though I am often in the depths of misery, there is still calmness, pure harmony and music inside me. I see paintings or drawings in the poorest cottages, in the dirtiest corners. And my mind is driven towards these things with an irresistible momentum.

Other things increasingly lose their hold on me, and the more they do so the more quickly my eye lights on the picturesque. Art demands dogged work, work in spite of everything and continuous observation. By dogged, I mean in the first place incessant labour, but also not abandoning one's views upon the say-so of this person or that.

I am not without hope, brother, that in a few years' time, or perhaps even now, little by little you will be seeing things I have done that will give you some satisfaction after all your sacrifices.

[*] In spite of everything

I have had singularly little discourse with painters lately. I haven't been the worse for it. It isn't the language of painters so much as the language of nature that one should heed. I can understand better now than I could a good six months ago why Mauve said: don't talk to me about Dupré, I'd rather you talked about the bank of that ditch, or something of the sort. That may sound a bit strong, and yet it is absolutely right. The feeling for things themselves, for reality, is of greater importance than the feeling for painting; anyway it is more productive and more inspiring.

Because I now have such a broad, such an expansive feeling for art and for life itself, of which art is the essence, it sounds so shrill and false when people like Tersteeg do nothing but harry one.

For my own part, I find that many modern pictures have a peculiar charm which the old ones lack. To me, one of the highest and noblest expressions of art will always be that of the English, for instance Millais and Herkomer and Frank Holl. What I would say with respect to the difference between old & present-day art is – perhaps the modern artists are deeper thinkers.

There is a great difference in sentiment between, for instance, Chill October by Millais and Bleaching Ground at Overveen by Ruysdael. And equally between Irish Emigrants by Holl and the women reading from the Bible by Rembrandt. Rembrandt & Ruysdael are sublime, for us as well as for their contemporaries, but there is something in the moderns that seems to us more personal and intimate.

It is the same with Swain's woodcuts & those of the old German masters.

And so it was a mistake when the modern painters thought it all the rage to imitate the old ones a few years ago. That's why I think old Millet is so right to say, 'Il me semble absurde que les hommes veuillent paraître autre chose que ce qu'ils sont.'[*] That may sound trite, and yet it is as unfathomably deep as the ocean, and personally I am all for taking it to heart.

I just wanted to tell you that I am going to get back to working regularly again, and must do so quand même[†] – and I'd just like to add that I look forward so much to a letter – and for the rest, I bid you good-night. Goodbye, with a handshake,

Ever yours,
Vincent

Please remember the <u>thick</u> Ingres if you can, enclosed is another sample. I still have a supply of the thin kind. I can do watercolour washes on the <u>thick Ingres</u>, but on the sans fin,[‡] for instance, it always goes blurry, which isn't entirely my fault.

---

[*] It seems absurd to me that people want to seem other than they are

[†] At that

[‡] Endless. Van Gogh was probably referring to 'paper on a roll' of a certain standard thickness.

I hope that by <u>keeping hard at it</u> I shall draw the little cradle another hundred times, besides what I did today.

228 [D]

Sunday morning
[3 September 1882]

My dear Theo,

I have just received your very welcome letter, and as I am taking a bit of a rest today, am answering it right away. Thank you very much for it and for the enclosure, and for the various things you say in it.

And many thanks for your description of that scene with the workmen in Montmartre, which I found very interesting because you convey the colours so well that I can see them. I am glad you are reading the book on Gavarni. I found it very interesting and it made me love G. twice as much.

Paris & its environs may be beautiful, but we have no complaints here either.

This week I did a painting that I think would remind you a little of Scheveningen as we saw it when we walked there together. A large study of sand, sea and sky – a big sky of delicate grey & warm white, with a single small patch of soft blue shimmering through – the sand & the sea light, so that the whole becomes golden, but animated by the boldly and distinctively coloured small figures and fishing smacks, which tend to set the tonal values. The subject of the sketch I made of it is a fishing smack weighing anchor. The horses stand ready for hitching up before pulling the smack into the sea. I am enclosing a small sketch of it.

It was really hard to do, I just wish I'd painted it on panel or on canvas. I tried to get more colour into it, that is, depth, strength of colour.

How strange it is that you & I so often seem to have the same thoughts. Yesterday evening, for instance, I came home from the woods with a study, having been deeply preoccupied with the question of depth of colour the whole week, and particularly at that moment. And I should very much have liked to have talked to you about it, especially with reference to the study I had done – and lo and behold, in this morning's letter you chance to mention that you were struck by the very vivid, yet harmonious, colours of Montmartre. I don't know if it was precisely the same thing that struck the two of us, but I do know that you would most certainly have been affected by what struck me so particularly and would probably have seen it in the same light.

As a start, I am sending you a small sketch of the subject and I shall tell you what the problem was. The woods are becoming thoroughly autumnal, and there are colour effects I don't often see in Dutch paintings.

Yesterday evening I was working on a slightly rising woodland slope covered with dry, mouldering beech leaves. The ground was light and dark reddish-brown, emphasized by the weaker and stronger shadows of trees casting half-obliterated stripes across it. The problem, and I found it a very difficult one, was to get the depth of colour, the enormous power & solidity of that ground – and yet it was only while I was painting it that I noticed how much light there was still in the dusk – to retain the light as well as the glow, the depth of that rich colour, for there is no carpet imaginable as splendid as that deep brownish-red in the glow of an autumn evening sun, however toned down by the trees.

Young beech trees spring from the ground, catching the light to one side, where they are a brilliant green, and the shadow side of the trunks is a warm, intense black-green.

Behind those saplings, behind that brownish-red ground, is a sky of a very delicate blue-grey, warm, hardly blue at all, sparkling. And against it there is a hazy border of greenness and a network of saplings and yellowish leaves. A few figures of wood gatherers are foraging about, dark masses of mysterious shadows. The white bonnet of a woman bending down to pick up a dry branch stands out suddenly against the deep reddish-brown of the ground. A skirt catches the light, a shadow is cast, the dark silhouette of a man appears above the wooded slope. A white bonnet, a cap, a shoulder, the bust of a woman show up against the sky. These figures, which are large and full of poetry, appear in the twilight of the deep shadowy tone like enormous terres cuites* taking shape in a studio.

* Terracottas

I am describing nature to you – I'm not sure to what extent I reproduced it in my sketch, but I do know that I was struck by the harmony of green, red, black, yellow, blue, brown, grey. It was very De Groux-like, an effect like, say, that sketch of Le depart du conscrit, formerly in the Palais Ducal.

It was a hard job painting it. The ground used up one and a half large tubes of white – even though the ground is very dark – and for the rest red, yellow, brown, ochre, black, sienna, bistre, and the result is a reddish-brown, but one ranging from bistre to deep wine-red and to a pale, golden ruddiness. Then there are still the mosses and a border of fresh grass which catches the light and glitters brightly and is very difficult to capture. So there in the end you have it, a sketch that I maintain has some significance, something to tell, whatever may be said about it.

I said to myself while I was doing it: don't let me leave before there is something of the autumnal evening in it, something mysterious, something important. However – because this effect doesn't last – I had to paint quickly, putting the figures in all at once, with a few forceful strokes of a firm brush. It had struck me how firmly the saplings were planted in the ground – I started on them with the brush, but because the ground was already impasted, brush strokes simply vanished into it. Then I squeezed roots and trunks in from the tube and modelled them a little with the brush.

Well, they are in there now, springing out of it, standing strongly rooted in it.

In a way I am glad that I never <u>learned</u> painting. In all probability I would then have learned to ignore such effects as this. Now I can say to myself, this is just what I want. If it is impossible, it is impossible, but I'm going to try it even though I don't know how it ought to be done. <u>I don't know myself</u> how I paint it, I just sit down with a white board in front of the spot that appeals to me, I look at what is in front of my eyes, and I say to myself: that white board has got to turn into something – I come back, dissatisfied, I lay it to one side and when I have rested a bit, I go and look at it with a kind of awe. Then I am still dissatisfied, because I have that splendid scenery too much in mind to be satisfied. Yet I can see in my work an echo of what appealed to me, I can see that the scenery has told me something, has spoken to me and that I have taken it down in short-hand. My shorthand may contain words that cannot be deciphered, mistakes or gaps, and yet there is something left of what the wood or the beach or the figure has told me, and it isn't in tame or conventional language derived from a studied manner or from some system, but from nature herself.

Enclosed another little sketch from the dunes. There are small bushes there whose leaves are white on one side, dark green on the other side & are constantly moving & glittering. Beyond them dark trees.

You can see that I am plunging full speed ahead into painting, I am plunging into colour. I have refrained from doing so up till now & am not sorry for it. Had I not already done some drawing, I should be unable to get the feeling of, or be able to tackle, a figure that looks like an unfinished terre cuite. But now that I sense I have gained the open sea, painting must go full speed ahead as fast as we are able.

If I am going to work on panel or canvas, then the expenses will go up again, everything is so expensive, paint is expensive, too, and so quickly used up. Well, these are complaints all painters have, we must see what can be done. I know for certain that I have a feeling for colour and shall acquire more & more, that painting is in the very marrow of my bones.

I value your loyal and effective help more than I can say. I think of you so much; I should so like my work to become vigorous, serious, virile, so that you too may get some pleasure from it as soon as possible.

One thing I should like to bring to your attention as a matter of importance – wouldn't it be possible to obtain paint, panels, brushes, &c, at <u>discount</u> prices? I am having to pay the <u>retail</u> price at the moment. Have you any connection with Paillard or someone like that? If so, I think it would be much more economical to get paints, say, wholesale, for instance white, ochre, sienna, and we could then come to some arrangement about the money. Everything would be cheaper, it goes without saying. Do think it over.

One doesn't paint well by using a lot of paint, but in order to do a ground effectively or to get a sky bright, one must sometimes not spare the tube. Sometimes the subject calls for less paint, sometimes the material, the nature of the subjects themselves, demands impasto.

Mauve, who paints very frugally in comparison with J. Maris and even more so in comparison with Millet or Jules Dupré, nevertheless has cigar boxes fall of the remnants of tubes in the corners of his studio, as plentiful as the empty bottles in the corners of rooms after a soirée or dinner such as Zola describes, for instance.

Well, if there could be a little extra this month, that would be wonderful. If not, then not. I shall work as hard as I can. You ask about my health, but what about yours? I would imagine my remedy would be yours as well: to be out in the open, painting. I am well, I still feel like it even when I'm tired, and that is getting better rather than worse. It's also a good thing, I think, that I live as frugally as possible, but my main remedy is painting.

I sincerely hope that your luck is in and that you will have even more. Please accept a handshake in my thoughts, and believe me,

Ever yours,

<u>Vincent</u>

You will see that there is a soft, golden effect in the little marine sketch and a more sombre, more serious mood in the woods. I am glad that both exist in life.

237 [D]

Sunday afternoon
[22 October 1882]

My dear Theo,

I don't need to tell you how delighted I was with your letter & the enclosure, it comes just in time and will be of tremendous help to me.

We are having autumn weather here, rainy & chilly, but full of atmosphere, especially good for figures, which stand out in tone against the wet streets and roads reflecting the sky. It is what Mauve, in particular, does so beautifully time and again. So I have been able to do some work on the large watercolour of the crowd of people in front of the lottery office, and I have also started another one of the beach, of which this is the composition.

I entirely agree with what you say about those times now and then when one feels dull-witted in the face of nature or when nature seems to have stopped speaking to us.

I get the same feeling quite often and it sometimes helps if I then tackle something quite different. When I feel jaded with landscapes or light effects, I tackle figures, and vice versa. Sometimes there is nothing for it but to wait for it to pass, but many a time I manage to do away with the numbness by changing my subject-matter.

However, I am becoming more and more fascinated by the figure. I remember there used to be a time when my feeling for landscape was very strong and I was much more impressed by a painting or drawing which captured a light effect or the atmosphere of a landscape than I was by the figure. Indeed, figure painters in general filled me with a kind of cool respect rather than with warm sympathy.

However, I remember very well being most impressed by a drawing of Daumier's: an old man under the chestnut trees in the Champs Elysées (an illustration for Balzac), though the drawing was not all that important. What impressed me so much at the time was something so stout and manly in Daumier's conception, something that made me think it must be good to think and to feel like that and to overlook or ignore a multitude of things and to concentrate on what makes us sit up and think and what touches us as human beings more directly and personally than meadows or clouds.

That is also why I always feel attracted to the figures of both the English draughtsmen and of the English writers, whose Monday-morning-like soberness and studied restraint and prose and analysis is something solid and substantial to which one can hang on in days when one feels weak. Among French writers the same is true of Balzac & Zola.

I don't know the books by Murger you mention but I hope to become acquainted with them. Did I tell you that I was reading Daudet's Les rois en exil? I thought it rather good.

The titles of those books greatly appeal to me, for instance, La bohème. How far we have strayed these days from la bohème of Gavarni's time! It seems to me that there was definitely something warmer and more light-hearted and alive about those days than there is today. But I cannot be certain, and there is much good nowadays, or there could be much more than in fact there is if there were greater solidarity.

At the moment I can see a splendid effect out of my studio window. The city, with its towers and roofs and smoking chimneys, is outlined as a dark, sombre silhouette against a horizon of light. This light is, however, no more than a broad streak over which hangs a heavy raincloud, more concentrated below, torn above by the autumn wind into large shreds & lumps that are being chased away. But that streak or light is making the wet roofs glisten here & there in the dark mass of the city (on a drawing one would achieve this with a stroke of body colour), so that although the mass has a single tone one can still distinguish between red tiles & slates. The Schenkweg runs through the foreground like a glistening streak through the wetness, the poplars have yellow leaves, the banks of the ditches & the meadows are a deep green, the little figures are black. I would have drawn it, or rather tried to draw it, had I not been working hard all afternoon on figures of peat-carriers, which are still too much on my mind to allow room for anything new, and should be allowed to linger.

I long for you so often and think of you so much. What you tell me about the character of some artists in Paris, who live with women, are less narrow-minded than others, perhaps trying desperately to preserve something youthful, I think is shrewdly observed indeed. Such people can be found here as well. It may be even more difficult over there than it is here to preserve some freshness in one's daily life, because to do so there means swimming even more against the tide. How many have not become desperate in Paris – calmly, rationally, logically and rightly desperate. I have been reading something of that sort about Tassaert, whom I like very much, and I feel sorry that this was what happened to him.

All the more, all the more do I consider every effort in that direction worthy of respect. I also think it is possible to achieve success without having to start out with despair. Even though one loses out here and there, and even though one sometimes feels a falling off, one must rally and take courage again, even though things should turn out differently from what one originally intended.

Please don't think that I look with contempt on such persons as you describe, just because their lives are not based on serious and well-considered principles. My opinion on the matter is this: what matters is deeds, not some abstract idea. I only approve of principles and think them worth the trouble if they turn into deeds, and I think it is good to reflect and to try to be conscientious, because this concentrates a man's energies and combines his various actions into a whole. The people you describe would, I believe, be more resolute if they thought more clearly about what they were going to do, but for the rest I greatly prefer the likes of them to people who parade their principles without taking the slightest trouble or even thinking about putting them into practice. For the latter gain nothing from the most beautiful principles and the former are precisely the people who, if they come round to living with resolve and thoughtfulness, might do something great. For great things do not just happen by impulse but are a succession of small things linked together.

What is drawing? How does one come to it? It is working through an invisible iron wall that seems to stand between what one _feels_ and what one _can do_. How is one to get through that wall – since pounding at it is of no use? In my opinion one has to undermine that wall, filing through it steadily and patiently. And there you are – how can one continue such work assidu[*] without being distracted or diverted, unless one reflects and orders one's life by principles? And as it is with art so it is with other things. And great things are not something accidental, they must be distinctly _willed_.

Whether a man's deeds originate in his principles or his principles in his deeds is something that seems to me as indeterminable (and as little worthy of determination) as the question of which came first, the chicken or the egg. But I consider that trying to develop one's power of thought and will is something positive and of much moment.

I am very curious to know what you will make of the figures I am doing these days, when you eventually

* Assiduously

see them. That poses another chicken-&-egg question: must one do figures for a previously planned composition, or combine figures that one has done separately so that they give rise to a composition? It seems to me that it probably comes down to the same thing, <u>provided only that one keeps working</u>.

I conclude with the same thing you said at the end of your letter, that we share a liking for peering behind the scenes, or, in other words, we have a tendency to analyse things. Now I believe that this is precisely the quality one has to have in order to paint – the strength one must exert in painting or drawing. It may be that nature has favoured us to some extent (in any case you and I certainly have it – perhaps we owe it to our boyhood in Brabant and to surroundings that taught us to think more than is usual), but it is really and truly not until later that the artistic sensibility develops and matures through work. I cannot tell you <u>how</u> you might become a very good painter, but that you have it in you and can bring it out is something I really do believe. Goodbye, my dear fellow, thank you for what you sent me and an affectionate handshake,

Ever yours,
Vincent

I have already lit my small stove. My dear fellow, how I wish we could just spend an evening together looking at drawings & sketches, and <u>woodcuts</u>, I have some splendid new ones. I hope to get some boys from the orphanage to pose for me this week, I might yet be able to save that drawing of orphans.

309 [D] [POSTSCRIPT]

[c. 4–8 August 1883]

[. . .]

For no particular reason, I cannot help adding a thought that often occurs to me. Not only did I start drawing relatively late in life, but it may well be that I shall not be able to count on many more years of life either.

If I think about it dispassionately – as if making calculations for an estimate or a specification – then it is in the nature of things that I cannot possibly know anything definite about it.

But by comparison with various people with whose lives one may be familiar, or by comparison with some with whom one is supposed to have some things in common, one can draw certain conclusions that are not completely without foundation.

So, as to the time I still have ahead of me for work, I think I may safely presume that my body will hold up for a certain number of years <u>quand bien même</u>[*] – a certain number between 6 and 10, say. (I can assume this the more safely as there is for the time being no immediate quand bien même.)

[*] In spite of everything

This is the period on which I count <u>firmly</u>. For the rest, it would be speculating far too wildly for me to dare make any definite pronouncements about myself, seeing that it depends precisely on those first, say, 10 years as to whether or not there will be anything after that time.

If one wears oneself out during these years then one won't live beyond 40. If one conserves enough strength to withstand the sort of shocks that tend to befall one, and manages to deal with various more or less complicated physical problems, then by the age of 40 to 50 one is back on a new, relatively normal course.

But such calculations are <u>not relevant at present</u>. Instead, as I started to say, one should plan for a period of between 5 and 10 years. I do not intend to spare myself, to avoid emotions or difficulties – it makes comparatively little difference to me whether I go on living for a shorter or longer time – besides I am not competent to manage my constitution the way, say, a physician is able to. And so I go on like an <u>ignoramus</u>, one who knows just one thing: <u>within a few years I must have done a certain amount of work</u> – I don't need to <u>rush</u>, for there is no point in that, but I must <u>carry on working</u> in complete calm and serenity, as regularly and with as much concentration as possible, as much to the point as possible. The world concerns me only in so far as I owe it a certain <u>debt</u> and <u>duty</u>, so to speak, because I have walked this earth for 30 years, and out of gratitude would like to leave some memento in the form of drawings and paintings – not made to please this school or that, but to express a genuine human feeling. So that work is my aim – and when one concentrates on this notion, everything one does is simplified, in that it isn't muddled but has a single objective. At present the work is going slowly – one reason more not to lose any time.

Guillaume Regamey was, I think, someone who left behind no particular reputation (you know that there are two Regameys, F. Regamey paints Japanese people and is his brother), but is nevertheless a personality for whom I have great respect. He died at the age of 38, and one period of his life lasting for 6 or 7 years was almost exclusively devoted to drawings with a highly distinct-ive style, done while he worked under some physical handicap. He is one of many – a very good one among many good ones.

I don't mention him to compare myself with him, I am not as good as he was, but to cite a specific example of self-control and willpower, sustained by one inspir-ing idea, which in difficult circumstances nevertheless showed him how to do good work with utter serenity.

That is how I regard myself, as having to accomplish in a few years something full of heart and love, and to do it with a will. Should I live longer, tant mieux,* but I put that out of my mind. <u>Something must be accomplished</u> in those few years, this thought guides all my plans. You will understand better now why I have a yearning to press on – and at the same time some determination to use simple means. And perhaps you will also be able to understand that as far as I am concerned I do not

* So much the better

consider my studies in isolation but always think of my work as a whole.

Nuenen

404 [D]

[c. 30 April 1885]

My dear Theo,

My warmest good wishes for good health & peace of mind on your birthday. I should have liked to send the painting of the Potato Eaters for this day, but although it's coming along well, it isn't quite finished yet.

Though the actual painting will have been completed in a comparatively short time, and largely from memory, it has taken a whole winter of painting studies of heads & hands.

And as for the few days in which I have painted it now – it's been a tremendous battle, but one for which I was filled with great enthusiasm. Even though at times I was afraid it would never come off. But painting, too, is 'agir-créer'.*

When weavers weave that cloth which I think they call cheviot, or those curious multicoloured Scottish tartan fabrics, then they try, as you know, to get strange broken

* Acting-creating

colours and greys into the cheviot – and to get the most vivid colours to balance each other in the multicoloured chequered cloth – so that instead of the fabric being a jumble, the <u>effet produit</u>* of the pattern looks harmonious from a distance.

A grey woven from red, blue, yellow, off-white & black threads – a blue broken by a green and an orange, red or yellow thread – are quite unlike <u>plain</u> colours, that is, they are more vibrant, and primary colours seem <u>hard</u>, cold and <u>lifeless</u> beside them.

Yet the weaver, or rather the designer, of the pattern or the colour combination does not always find it easy to make an exact estimate of the number of threads and their direction – no more than it is easy to weave brush strokes into a harmonious whole.

If you could see the first painted studies I did on my arrival here in Nuenen side by side with the canvas I am doing now, I think you would agree that things are livening up a bit as far as colour is concerned.

I feel certain that you too will get involved in the question of colour analysis one day. For as an art connoisseur and critic, it seems to me, one must also <u>be sure</u> of one's ground and have firm <u>convictions</u> – for one's own pleasure at least, and in order to <u>substantiate one's opinion</u>. And one should also be able to explain it in a few words to others who sometimes turn to someone like yourself for information when they want to know a little more about art.

* Overall effect

But now I have something to say about Portier. Of course I am not wholly indifferent to his private opinion and I also appreciate his saying that he does not take back anything of what he has said. Nor do I mind that he apparently failed to hang these first studies. But – if he wants me to send him a painting intended for him, then he can only have it on condition that he shows it.

As for the Potato Eaters – it is a painting that will do well in gold – of that I am certain. But it would do just as well on a wall papered in a deep shade of ripe corn. However, it simply mustn't be seen without being set off in this way. It will not appear to full advantage against a dark background and especially not against a dull background. And that is because it is a glimpse into a very grey interior. In real life it is also set in a gold frame, as it were, because the hearth and the light from the fire on the white walls would be nearer the spectator – they are situated outside the painting, but in its natural state the whole thing is projected backwards.

Once again, it must be set off by putting something coloured a deep gold or copper round it. Please bear that in mind if you want to see it as it should be seen. Associating it with a gold tone lends brightness to areas where you would least expect it, and at the same time does away with the marbled aspect it assumes if it is unfortunately placed against a dull or black background. The shadows are painted with blue and the gold colour sets this off.

Yesterday, I took it to a friend of mine in Eindhoven who is doing some painting. In about 3 days' time I'll go back over there and give it some egg-white and finish off a few details.

This man, who is trying very hard himself to learn how to paint and to handle colour, was particularly taken with it. He had already seen the study on which I had based the lithograph and said that he would never have believed I could improve the colour and the drawing to such an extent. As he, too, paints from the model, he is well aware of what there is to a peasant's head or fist, and as for the hands, he said that he now had a quite different understanding of how to do them.

The point is that I've tried to bring out the idea that these people eating potatoes by the light of their lamp have dug the earth with the self-same hands they are now putting into the dish, and it thus suggests <u>manual labour</u> and – a meal honestly <u>earned</u>. I wanted to convey a picture of a way of life quite different from ours, from that of civilized people. So the last thing I would want is for people to admire or approve of it without knowing why.

I've held the threads of this fabric in my hands all winter long and searched for the definitive pattern – and although it is now a fabric of rough and coarse appearance, the threads have none the less been chosen with care and according to certain rules. And it might just turn out to be a <u>genuine peasant painting</u>. <u>I know that it is</u>. But anyone who prefers to have his peasants looking namby-pamby had best suit himself. Personally, I am convinced that in the long run one gets better results from painting them in all their coarseness than from introducing a conventional sweetness.

A peasant girl, in her patched and dusty blue skirt & bodice which have acquired the most delicate shades from the weather, wind and sun, is better looking – in my opinion – than a lady. But if she dons a lady's clothes, then her authenticity is gone. A peasant in his fustian clothes out in the fields [is] better looking than when he goes to church on Sundays in a kind of gentleman's coat.

And similarly, in my opinion, it would be wrong to give a painting of peasant life a conventional polish. If a peasant painting smells of bacon, smoke, potato steam, fine – that's not unhealthy – if a stable reeks of manure – all right, that's what a stable is all about – if a field has the smell of ripe corn or potatoes or of guano & manure – that's properly healthy, especially for city dwellers. Such pictures might prove <u>helpful to them</u>. But a painting of peasant life should not be perfumed.

I am eager to know whether you will find something in it to please you – I hope so.

I'm glad that just as Mr Portier has said that he'll handle my work, I've got something more important for him than studies. As for Durand Ruel – though he didn't consider the drawings worth bothering with, do show him this painting. Let him think it ugly, I don't mind – but let him have a look at it all the same, let people see that we put some effort into our endeavours. No doubt you'll hear 'quelle croûte!'* Be prepared for that, as I am prepared myself. Yet we must go on providing something <u>genuine</u> and <u>honest</u>.

* What a daub!

Painting peasant life is a serious business, and I for one would blame myself if I didn't try to make pictures that give rise to serious reflection in those who think seriously about art and life.

Millet, De Groux, so many others, have set an example of <u>character</u> by turning a deaf ear to such taunts as 'sale, grassier, boueux, puant',* &c, &c, so it would be a disgrace should one so much as waver. No, one must paint peasants as if one were one of them, as if one felt and thought as they do. Being unable to help what one actually is. I very often think that peasants are a world apart, in many respects one so much better than the civilized world. Not in all respects, for what do they know of art and many other things?

I still have a few smaller studies – but you will appreciate that I'm being kept so busy by the larger one that I've been able to do little else. As soon as it is completely finished and dry, I shall forward you the canvas in a small packing case, adding a few smaller items. I think it would be as well not to delay the dispatch too long, which is why I'll make haste with it. The second lithograph of it will probably have to be abandoned in that case, though I realize that Mr Portier, for instance, must have his opinion endorsed if we are to count on him once and for all as a friend. It is my sincere hope that we may.

I have been so absorbed in the painting that I almost forgot that I am moving house, something that has to be attended to as well. My worries won't be any the less,

* Nasty, crude, filthy, stinking

but the lives of all painters in this genre have been so full of cares that I shouldn't want to have things any easier than they did. And since they managed to get their paintings done anyway, I, too, may be <u>held back</u> by material difficulties, but not <u>destroyed</u> or <u>undermined</u> by them. So there you are.

I believe that <u>The Potato Eaters</u> will turn out well – as you know, the last few days are always tricky with a painting because before it's completely dry one can't use a large brush without running a real risk of spoiling it. And changes must be made very coolly and calmly with a small brush. That's why I took it to my friend and asked him to make certain I didn't spoil it, and why I'll be going to his place to apply those finishing touches.

You'll certainly see that it has originality. Regards, I'm sorry it wasn't ready for today – best wishes once again for your health and peace of mind, believe me, with a handshake,

Ever yours,

<u>Vincent</u>

I'm still working on some smaller studies that will go off at the same time. Did you ever send that copy of the Salon issue?

Antwerp

437 [D]

[28 November 1885]

My dear Theo,

I just wanted to send you a few more impressions of Antwerp. This morning I took a good long walk in the pouring rain, the object of the outing being to fetch my things from the custom house. The various warehouses and storage sheds on the quays look quite splendid.

I've walked in many different directions along the docks & quays several times already. The contrast is particularly marked for one who has just arrived from the sand and the heath & the tranquillity of a country village and has been in quiet surroundings for a long time. It's all an impenetrable confusion.

One of de Goncourt's sayings was, 'Japonaiserie for ever.' Well, those docks are one huge Japonaiserie, fantastic, peculiar, unheard of – or at any rate, that's one way of looking at them. I would love to take a walk there in your company some day, just to find out if we see things in the same way.

Everything could be done there, townscapes, figures of the most diverse character, ships as the main subject with water & the sky a delicate grey – but, above all – Japonaiseries. The point I'm trying to make is that there are always figures in motion there, one sees them in the strangest setting, everything looks fantastic, with interesting contrasts at every turn. A white horse in the mud in a corner where piles of merchandise lie covered with a tarpaulin – against the old, black, smoke-stained walls of the warehouse. Perfectly simple, but with a Black & White effect.

Through the window of a very elegant English public house one can look out on the filthiest mud and on a ship from which, say, such pleasing wares as hides and buffalo horns are being unloaded by docker types as ugly as sin, or by exotic sailors, while a very fair, very delicate English girl stands at the window looking out at this or at something else. The interior with figure wholly in tone, and for light – the silvery sky above the mud and the buffalo horns – again a series of fairly strong contrasts.

Flemish sailors with excessively ruddy faces and broad shoulders, lusty and tipsy, Antwerpers through & through, are to be seen eating mussels or drinking beer with a great deal of noise and commotion. In contrast – there goes a tiny little figure in black, small hands clasped close to her body, scuttling noiselessly past the grey walls. In an encadrement* of jet-black hair, a small oval face. Brown? Orange-yellow? I'm not sure. For a moment she looks up and gives a slanting glance from a pair of jet-black eyes. She is a Chinese girl, quiet as a mouse, stealthy, small, naturally bedbug-like. What a contrast to the group of Flemish mussel-eaters!

* Frame

Another contrast – one walks down a very narrow street between tremendously tall buildings, warehouses and storehouses. But at ground level in the street – alehouses for every nationality, with males and females to match, shops for food, for seamen's clothing, colourful and bustling. The street is long, at every turn one sees a typical scene, a commotion, perhaps, more intense than usual, as a squabble breaks out. For example, there you are walking along, just looking around – and suddenly cheers go up and there's a lot of yelling. A sailor is being thrown out of a brothel by the girls in broad daylight and is being pursued by a furious fellow and a string of prostitutes, of whom he seems to be terrified – anyway, I see him clamber over a pile of sacks and disappear through a window into a warehouse.

When one has had enough of this hullaballoo – with the city behind one at the end of the landing stages where the Harwich and Havre steamers lie, there is nothing, absolutely nothing to be seen in front except for an infinite expanse of flat, half-flooded pasture, immensely melancholy and wet, with undulating dry reeds, and mud – the river with a single small black boat, water in the foreground grey, sky misty and cold, grey – still as the desert.

As to the overall impression of the harbour, or of one of the docks – at one moment it is more tangled and fantastic than a thorn hedge, so chaotic that one finds no rest for the eye, grows giddy, and is forced by the 'papillot-ering'*

* Flickering

of colours and lines to look first here, then there, unable to distinguish one thing from another – even after looking at the same point for a long time. But if one moves on to a certain spot with an undefined stretch of land in the foreground, then one again encounters the most beautiful, most peaceful lines and those effects which Mols, for instance, so often achieves.

Here one may see a splendidly healthy-looking girl, who is, or at least seems, wholly honest and unaffectedly cheerful; there a face so slyly vicious, like a hyena's, that it frightens one. Not to forget faces ravaged by small-pox, the colour of boiled shrimps, with dull, grey little eyes, no eyebrows and sparse, greasy, thinning hair the colour of pure hog bristle, or a bit yellower – Swedish or Danish types.

I'd like to do some work round there, but how and where, for one would get into trouble exceedingly quickly. All the same I've roamed through quite a number of streets & alleyways without mishap, have even sat down to talk in a very friendly way with various girls, who seemed to take me for a bargee.

I think it not unlikely that painting portraits may help me to come by some good models. I got my gear today, and some materials, to which I'd been looking forward very eagerly. So now my studio is all ready. If I could come by a good model for a song, I'd be afraid of nothing. Nor do I mind very much that I haven't enough money to force the pace. Perhaps the idea of doing portraits and getting the subjects to pay for them by posing is a safer method. You see, in the city things aren't the same as when one deals with peasants.

Well, one thing is certain, Antwerp is a splendid and very remarkable place for a painter.

My studio isn't at all bad, especially now that I've pinned up a lot of small Japanese prints which I enjoy very much. You know, those small female figures in gardens or on the beach, horsemen, flowers, gnarled thorn branches.

I'm glad I came here – and hope not to sit still and do nothing this winter. Anyway, it's a relief to have a small hideaway where I can work when the weather is bad. It goes without saying that I won't be living in the lap of luxury.

Try to send your letter off on the first, for while I've enough to live on until then, I shall be getting the wind up after that.

My little room has turned out better than I expected and certainly doesn't look dreary.

Now that I have the 3 studies I took along with me here, I shall try to make contact with the marchands de tableaux,* who seem, however, to live for the most part in private houses, with no display windows giving on to the street.

The park is beautiful too. I sat there one morning and did some drawing.

Well – I've had no setbacks so far, and I'm well off as far as accommodation is concerned, for by sacrificing

* Picture dealers

another few francs I've acquired a stove and a lamp. I shan't easily get bored, believe me.

I've also found Lhermitte's <u>Octobre</u>, women in a potato field in the evening, splendid, but not his Novembre yet. Have you kept track of that by any chance? I've also seen that there's a Figaro illustré with a beautiful drawing by Raffaëlli.

My address, as you know, is 194 Rue des images, so please send your letter there, and the second de Goncourt volume when you've finished with it. Regards,

Ever yours,
<u>Vincent</u>

It's odd that my painted studies look darker here in the city than in the country. Is that because the light isn't as bright in the city? I'm not sure, but it might matter more than one might think at first sight. I was struck by it and can imagine that some of the things that are with you now also look darker than I thought they were in the country. Yet those I brought along with me don't seem the worse for it – the mill, avenue with autumn trees, a still life, as well as a few small things.

Paris

462 [F]

Paris [summer 1887]

My dear friend,

Thank you for your letter, and for what it contained. It saddens me to think that even successful paintings do not cover their costs.

I was touched by what you wrote about the family. 'They are fairly well but even so it's sad to see them.' Twelve years ago one would have sworn that, come what may, the family would always get on and do well. It would give Mother much pleasure if your marriage came off, and you also ought not to stay single for the sake of your health and business. As for me – I feel the desire for marriage and children dwindling and now and then I'm rather depressed that I should be like that as I approach 35, when I ought to be feeling quite the opposite. And sometimes I blame it all on this rotten painting. It was Richepin who said somewhere: the love of art is the undoing of true love. I think that's absolutely right, but on the other hand true love makes one weary of art. And although I already feel old and broken, I can still be amorous enough at times to feel less passionate about painting. One must have ambition to succeed, and ambition seems to me absurd. I wish above all I were less of a burden to you – and that needn't be impossible from now on, for I hope to make such progress that you'll be able to show what I do in full confidence without compromising yourself. And then I'll retire somewhere down south and get away from the sight of so many painters who fill me with disgust as human beings.

You can be sure of one thing – I shan't be trying to do any more work for the Tambourin. Anyway, I think it's about to change hands, and I most certainly won't raise any objections to that. As for la Segatori, that is quite a different matter. I still feel affection for her and I hope that she, too, still feels some for me. But at the moment she is in a difficult situation, she is neither a free agent nor mistress in her own house, on top of which she's in pain and unwell. Although I wouldn't say so openly – I'm convinced she's had an abortion (unless, that is, she did have a miscarriage) – anyway, in her case I don't hold it against her.

She'll be better in about two months' time, I hope, and then she may well be grateful to me for not having bothered her. Mind you, once she's well again, if she refuses in cold blood to return what is mine, or does me down in any way, I shan't pull my punches – but it won't come to that. After all, I know her well enough to trust her still. And mind you, if she does manage to hang on to her establishment, then from a business point of view I shouldn't blame her for choosing to fleece rather than be fleeced. If that means she has to tread on my toes a bit – all right – she can get on with it. When I saw her last, she didn't tread all over my heart, which she would have done had she been as nasty as people say.

I saw Tanguy yesterday and he has put a canvas I've just done in the window. I've done four since you left and I've got a big one under way. I realize that these big, long canvases are hard to sell, but later on people will see that there's fresh air and good humour in them. The whole lot would do well as decoration for a dining room or a country house. And if you were to fall properly in love and were to get married, then it doesn't seem impossible to me that you might manage to acquire a country house like so many other art dealers. If one lives well, one spends more, but also gains more ground, and perhaps nowadays one does better looking rich than looking hard up. It's better to enjoy life than to do away with oneself. Regards to all at home.

Ever yours,
Vincent

II

The Best Days

Arles

468 [F]

[10 March 1888]

My dear Theo,

Thank you for your letter and the enclosed 100 fr. note.
I very much hope that Tersteeg will be coming to Paris
soon, as you seem to expect. It would be most welcome
with things in the state you say they're in, everyone with
their backs to the wall and in such financial straits. I'm
very interested in what you write about the Lançon sale
and the painter's mistress. He's done work of much indi-
viduality, his drawing often reminds me of Mauve's. I'm
sorry not to have seen the exhibition of his studies, just
as I also very much regret not having seen the Willette
exhibition.

What do you think of the news that Kaiser Wilhelm
has died? Will that speed things up in France, and will
Paris stay calm? It seems unlikely. And what effect will
all this have on the picture trade? I read that there seems
to be some talk of abolishing import duties on pictures
in America, is that true?

It might be easier to get a few dealers and art lovers
to agree to buy the impressionist pictures than to get

the artists to agree to equal shares in the price of the pictures sold.

Even so, the artists could not do better than combine forces, give their pictures to the association, and share the proceeds of any sales, the society thus guaranteeing that its members can go on living and working. If Degas, Claude Monet, Renoir, Sisley and C. Pissarro would take the initiative and say, Look here, the five of us will each hand over 10 pictures (or rather, we'll each hand over work to the value of 10,000 fr., estimated by expert members co-opted by the society such as Tersteeg and yourself, the said experts also investing capital in the form of pictures), and we furthermore undertake to hand pictures over every year to the value of . . . And we invite the rest of you, Guillaumin, Seurat, Gauguin, &c., &c., to join us (your pictures subjected to the same expert valuation).

Thus the great impressionists of the Grand Boulevard, by giving pictures that would become general property, would preserve their prestige, and the others would no longer be able to reproach them for keeping to themselves the advantages of a reputation no doubt acquired in the first place by their personal efforts and their individual talent – but in the second place also enhanced, consolidated and maintained by the paintings of a whole battalion of artists who have been working in unremitting poverty.

Be that as it may, it is to be hoped that this will come off and that Tersteeg and you will become the society's expert members (perhaps together with Portier?).

I've got two more landscape studies. I hope the work

will go on steadily from now on and that I'll be able to send you a first batch in a month – I say in a month, because I want to send you only the best, and because I want them to be dry, and because I want to send at least a dozen of them at a time, on account of the freight charges.

I congratulate you on the purchase of the Seurat – with what I'm going to send you, you might try to arrange another exchange with Seurat as well.

You do realize that if Tersteeg joins you in this business, the two of you could easily persuade Boussod & Valadon to grant a sizeable credit for the necessary purchases. But it is urgent, or else other dealers will pull the carpet from under your feet.

I've made the acquaintance of a Danish artist who talks about Heyerdahl and other people from the north, Kroyer, &c. What he does is dry, but very conscientious, and he is still young. He saw the impressionist exhibition in the Rue Lafitte some time ago. He'll probably come to Paris for the Salon, and wants to do a tour of Holland to see the museums.

I approve of your exhibiting the Books with the Indépendants – you should give this study the title 'Romans parisiens'.

I would be so glad to learn that you had managed to persuade Tersteeg – do be patient with him, anyway.

I had to get 50 frs.' worth of bits and pieces when your letter arrived. I'll be starting this week on 4 or 5 things.

I think every day about this artists' association, and the plan has developed further in my mind, but Tersteeg must be in on it, and much depends on that. Right now the painters would probably let themselves be persuaded by us, but we can get no further until we have Tersteeg's help. Without that we'd have to listen to the lamentations of one and all from morning to night and each one would be forever coming round individually demanding explanations and axioms, &c. I shouldn't be a bit surprised if Tersteeg took the view that one could not do without the artists of the Grand Boulevard – and that he will advise you to persuade them to take the initiative in the association by handing in pictures which would then become common property and cease to belong to them alone. A proposal which, in my opinion, the Petit Boulevard would be morally obliged to support.

And these gentlemen of the Grand Boulevard will only hold on to their present high reputation by forestalling the not unfounded criticisms of the lesser impressionists who will say, 'Everything goes into your own pocket.' To that they may well reply, 'Not at all, on the contrary, we are the first to say our pictures belong <u>to the artists</u>.' If Degas, Monet, Renoir and Pissarro were to say that – (even leaving plenty of latitude for their personal views on how best to implement the scheme) – they would be doing better than by saying nothing at all and letting things slide.

Yours,
Vincent

474 [F]

[9 April 1888]

My dear Theo,

Thank you for your letter and the enclosed 100 fr. note. I have sent you some sketches of the pictures intended for Holland. It goes without saying that the painted studies are more vivid in colour. Am hard at work again, still on orchards in bloom.

The air here is definitely doing me good, I wish you could fill your lungs with it. One of its effects on me is quite amusing, a single small glass of cognac here goes to my head, so without my having to use stimulants to make my blood circulate, my constitution is under less strain. The only thing is, I've had a terribly weak stomach ever since I arrived, but that's probably just a question of being patient.

I hope to make real progress this year which, to be sure, I badly need to do. I've got a new orchard which is as good as the pink peach trees – apricot trees of a very pale pink. At the moment I'm working on some plum trees, yellowy white, with thousands of black branches. I am using up an enormous amount of canvases and paints, but I hope it's not a waste of money for all that. Out of 4 canvases there'll be perhaps one at the most which will make a <u>picture</u>, like Tersteeg's or Mauve's, but the studies might come in useful as exchanges, I hope. When can I send you something? I'm very keen to do two of the one I did for Tersteeg, as it's better than the Asnières studies.

I saw another bullfight yesterday, where 5 men played the bull with banderillas and cockades. A toreador crushed one of his balls jumping the barricade. He was a fair man with grey eyes who showed great sang froid – they said he'll be laid up for a long time. He was dressed in sky blue and gold, exactly like the little horsemen in our Monticelli with the 3 figures in a wood. The bullrings are quite beautiful when there is sunshine and a crowd.

Good for Pissarro, I'm sure he's right. I hope he'll do an exchange with us one day. The same goes for Seurat. It would be a good deal getting a painted study by him. Anyway, I'm working hard, hoping we can bring something like this off.

It's going to be a hard month for you and me, but if you can possibly manage, it would be to our advantage to make the most of the orchards in bloom. I am into my stride at the moment and could do with another 10, I think, of the same subject.

You know I chop and change in my work, and this passion for painting orchards won't last for ever. After this it could be bullrings. Then I also have an <u>enormous</u> number of drawings to do, as I want to do some in the manner of Japanese prints. There's nothing like striking while the iron is hot. Shall be exhausted after the orchards, as the canvases are sizes 25 & 30 & 20. We could never have too many of them, even if I turned out double the amount.

It seems to me that this may well break the ice in Holland once and for all. Mauve's death was a severe blow to me. You will see that the pink peach trees were painted with some passion. I must also do a starry night with cypresses or – perhaps over a field of ripe corn. There are some extremely beautiful nights here. I am in a constant fever of work.

Am very curious to know what the result will be by the end of a year. I hope that by then I'll be less dogged by ill-health. At present I suffer quite a lot on some days, but am not in the least worried as it is merely a reaction to last winter, which was out of the ordinary. And my blood is coming right, that's the main thing.

We must get to the point where the value of my pictures covers my expenditure, and even exceeds it, in view of how much has already been spent. Oh well, it will come. I don't bring everything off, naturally, but the work is coming along. You haven't complained about what I've laid out so far, but I warn you that if I continue to work at the same rate I shall find it very hard to make ends meet. It's just that there is an inordinate amount of work.

If there is a month or a fortnight when you feel hard pressed, let me know – I'll immediately get down to some drawings, and that will cost us less. Just to tell you that you mustn't put yourself out without good reason – there is so much to do here, all kinds of studies, not as in Paris, where you can't even sit down where you want to.

If you could possibly manage to spare a bit extra for one month, so much the better, because orchards in bloom are the sort of thing that stand some chance of selling or exchanging. But I haven't forgotten that you have your rent to pay, that's why you must warn me if things get too tight.

I'm still going around all the time with the Danish painter, but he'll be leaving soon. He's an intelligent fellow, very dependable and well mannered, but his painting is still not up to much. You'll probably see him when he passes through Paris.

It was good of you to go to Bernard's. If he does his service in Algeria, who knows, perhaps I'll go there to keep him company. Is winter in Paris over at last?

I think what Kahn says is perfectly true, that I haven't taken tonal values into account enough, but they'll be saying something very different later on – no less true. It's impossible to deal with tonal values and colour. Th. Rousseau did it better than anyone else, but because of the mixing of the colours, the darkening with time has increased, and his pictures are now unrecognizable. One cannot be at the pole and the equator at the same time. One has to choose, which I hope I do, and it will probably be colour. Good-bye for now. A handshake to you, Koning and our friends,

Vincent

B7 [F] [LETTER FROM VINCENT TO
ÉMILE BERNARD]

[c. 18 June 1888]

My dear Bernard,

Forgive me for writing in haste, I'm afraid my letter will be illegible, but I did want to reply at once.

Do you realize that we have been very stupid, Gauguin, you and I, in not going to the same place? But when Gauguin left, I still wasn't sure if I could get away, and when you left, that awful money business, and the bad reports I sent you about the cost of living here, stopped you from coming.

It wouldn't have been such a stupid thing to do if we had all gone to Arles together, for with three of us here, we could have done our own housekeeping. And now that I have found my bearings a bit more, I am beginning to discover the advantages. For my part, I'm getting on better here than I did in the north. I even work right in the middle of the day, in the full sun, with no shade at all, out in the wheat fields, and lo and behold, I am as happy as a cicada. My God, if only I had known this country at 25 instead of coming here at 35! At that time I was fascinated by grey, or rather lack of colour. I kept dreaming of Millet, and then I also had such acquaintances among the Dutch painters as Mauve, Israëls, etc.

Here is a sketch of a sower: a large piece of land with

clods of ploughed earth, for the most part a definite purple. A field of ripe wheat, in yellow ochre with a little carmine.

The sky chrome yellow, almost as bright as the sun itself, which is chrome yellow 1 with a little white, while the rest of the sky is chrome yellow 1 and 2 mixed. Thus very yellow.

The Sower's smock is blue and his trousers white.

Size 25 canvas, square.

There are many touches of yellow in the soil, neutral tones produced by mixing purple with the yellow, but I couldn't care less what the colours are in <u>reality</u>. I'd sooner do those naïve pictures out of old almanacs, old farmers' almanacs where hail, snow, rain or fine weather are depicted in a wholly primitive manner, like the one Anquetin used so successfully in his Moisson. To be honest with you, I have absolutely no objection to the countryside, since I grew up in it – I am still enchanted by snatches of the past, have a hankering after the eternal, of which the sower and the sheaf of corn are the symbols. But when shall I ever get round to doing the <u>starry sky</u>, that picture which is always in my mind?

Alas, alas, it is just as the excellent fellow Cyprien says in J. K. Huysman's 'En ménage': the most beautiful paintings are those which you dream about when you lie in bed smoking a pipe, but which you never paint

Yet you have to make a start, no matter how incompetent you feel in the face of inexpressible perfection, of the overwhelming beauty of nature.

How I should like to see the study you have done of the brothel!

I am always reproaching myself for not having done any figures here yet.

Herewith another landscape. Setting sun? Rising moon?

A summer sun, anyway.

Town purple, celestial body yellow, sky green-blue. The wheat has all the hues of old gold, copper, green-gold or red-gold, yellow-gold, yellow-bronze, red-green. Size 30 canvas, square.

I painted it at the height of the mistral. My easel was fixed in the ground with iron pegs, a method I recommend to you. You push the legs of the easel deep into the ground, then drive iron pegs fifty centimetres long into the ground beside them. You tie the whole lot together with rope. This way you can work in the wind.

This is what I wanted to say about black and white. Take the Sower. The picture is divided in two; one half is yellow, the upper part, the lower part is purple. Well, the white trousers help rest the eye and distract it just as the excessive contrast of yellow and purple starts to jar. There you are, that's what I wanted to say.

I know a second lieutenant in the Zouaves here; his name is Milliet. I give him drawing lessons – with my perspective frame – and he is beginning to do some drawings and, honestly, I've seen far worse. He is keen to learn, has been in Tonkin, etc. . . . . He is leaving for Africa in October. If you were to join the Zouaves, he would take you along and guarantee you a fairly large measure of freedom to paint, at least if you were willing to help him with his artistic plans. Might this be of any use to you? If so, let me know as soon as possible.

One reason for working is that the canvases are worth money. Since you doubt that, you may call this reason fairly prosaic. But it is true. One reason for not working is that canvases and paint simply swallow up our money while they are waiting to be sold.

Drawings, on the other hand, don't cost a lot.

Gauguin too is bored at Pont-Aven, complains just like you of his isolation. If only you could go and see him! But I haven't any idea whether he means to stay, and I'm inclined to think he's planning to go to Paris. He told me he thought you would come to Pont-Aven. My God, if only all three of us were here! You will say that it's too out of the way. All right, but think of the winter, for here you can work all year round. The reason why I love this country is that I have less to fear from the cold, which, because it stops my blood circulating properly, makes it impossible for me to think or even do anything at all.

You will see that for yourself when you are a soldier. Then your melancholy will be gone, which could easily be the result of your having too little or the wrong blood, which I don't really think is the case.

It's the fault of that damned foul wine in Paris and those foul greasy steaks.

My God, I had reached the point where my blood was

no longer circulating at all, literally no longer at all. But after four weeks it has started to circulate again. However, my dear friend, at the same time I have had, just like you, a fit of melancholy, from which I would have suffered as much as you, had I not welcomed it with great pleasure as a sign that I was recovering – which is indeed what happened.

So, don't go back to Paris but stay in the countryside, for you will need your strength to come through the trial of serving in Africa. Well then, the more blood you produce beforehand, good blood, the better it will be, for over there in the heat you may not be able to do it quite so easily.

Painting and fucking a lot don't go together, it softens the brain. Which is a bloody nuisance.

The symbol of St Luke, the patron saint of painters, is, as you know, an ox. So you just be patient as an ox if you want to work in the artistic field. Still, bulls are lucky not to have to work at that foul business of painting.

But what I wanted to say is this: after the period of melancholy is over you will be stronger than before, you will recover your health, and you will find the scenery round you so beautiful that you will want to do nothing but paint.

I think that your poetry will change in the same way as your painting. After a few eccentric things, you have succeeded in doing some with Egyptian calm and a great simplicity.

'Que l'heure est done brève
Qu'on passe en aimant,
C'est moins qu'un instant,
Un peu plus qu'un rêve.
Le temps nous enlève
Notre enchantement.'*

That's not by Baudelaire, I don't know who wrote it. They're the words of a song found in Daudet's Nabab – that's where I took it from – but doesn't it express the idea just like a shrug of the shoulders from a real lady?

The other day I read Loti's Madame Chrysanthème, it includes interesting details about Japan.

My brother is holding a Claude Monet exhibition at the moment which I should very much like to see. Guy de Maupassant among others came to have a look, and said that he'll be coming often to the Boulevard Montmartre in the future.

I must go and paint, so I'll stop; I'll probably write again soon. A thousand apologies for my not putting enough stamps on that letter, even though I stuck them on at the post office, nor is this the first time that it has happened here that, being in doubt and enquiring at the counter, I have been given the wrong information about the postage. You have no idea of the indifference, the unconcern of the people here. Anyway, you'll soon be

* How short, then, the hour / One spends in loving, / It is less than an instant, / Little more than a dream. / Time strips us of / Our enchantment.

seeing all that with your own eyes, in Africa. Thanks for your letter, I hope to write again soon, at a moment when I'm in less of a rush. With a handshake,

Vincent

BII [F] [LETTER FROM VINCENT TO ÉMILE BERNARD]

[c. 17 July 1888]

My dear friend Bernard,

I've just sent you another 9 sketches after painted studies. So you'll see subjects from the scenery that inspires old man Cézanne, because the Crau near Aix is almost the same as the countryside round Tarascon or the Crau here. The Camargue is even plainer, for often there is nothing, nothing, other than poor soil and tamarisk bushes and the coarse grass that is to these bare pastures what esparto grass is to the desert.

Knowing how keen you are on Cézanne, I thought you might like these sketches of Provence; not that a drawing of mine and one by Cézanne have much in common. No, indeed, any more than Monticelli and I! But I too love the countryside they have loved so much, and for the same reasons, the colour and the logical composition.

My dear friend Bernard, by <u>collaboration</u> I did not mean to say that I think two or more painters would have to work on the same pictures. What I was driving at was paintings that differ from one another yet go together and complement one another.

Just take the Italian primitives or the German primitives or the Dutch school or the real Italians, in short, take the whole of the art of painting!

Whether they want it or not, their work forms a 'group', a 'series'.

Well, now, at present the impressionists also form a group, despite all their disastrous civil wars, in which both sides have been trying to get at each other's throats with a dedication they would have done better to reserve for other ends.

In our northern school, you have Rembrandt, who heads that school because his influence may be seen in anyone who comes to know him more closely. Thus we find Paulus Potter painting rutting and excited animals in equally exciting landscapes – in a thunderstorm, in the sunshine, in the melancholy of autumn – while that selfsame Paulus Potter, before he came to know Rembrandt, was rather dry and over-fussy.

Here are two people, Rembrandt and Potter, who belong together like brothers, and even though Rembrandt probably never touched a picture by Potter with his brush, that doesn't alter the fact that Potter and Ruysdael owe him all that is best in them – the thing that moves us so deeply when we have learned how to look at a corner of old Holland as if through their temperament.

Moreover, the material problems of the painter's life make it desirable that painters should collaborate and unite (much as they did in the days of the Guilds of St Luke). If only they would ensure their material well-being, and love one another like friends instead of making one another's life hell, painters would be happier, and in any case less ridiculous, less foolish and less culpable.

However, I shan't labour the point, because I realize that life carries us along so fast that we haven't the time to talk and to work as well. That is the reason why, with unity still a long way off, we are now sailing the trackless deep in our frail little boats, all alone on the high seas of our time.

Is it a renaissance? Is it a decline? We cannot judge, because we are too close to it not to be deceived by distorted perspectives. Contemporary events, our setbacks and successes, probably assume exaggerated proportions in our eyes.

A hearty handshake from me and I hope to hear something from you soon.

Ever yours,

Vincent

514 [F] [PART]

[c. 25 July 1888]

My dear Theo,

Thank you for your kind letter. If you remember, mine ended with 'we are getting old, that is the <u>fact of the matter</u>, and all the rest is <u>imagination</u> and simply does not exist'. Well, I said that more for myself than for you. And I said it because I feel it is absolutely essential for me to take action accordingly, not perhaps by working harder but with greater seriousness.

You mention the emptiness you sometimes feel, and that's exactly what I feel myself.

Consider, if you will, the times in which we live to be a true and great renaissance of art, the worm-ridden official tradition still holding sway yet ultimately impotent and idle, the new painters still isolated, poor, treated as madmen, and because of this treatment actually going insane, at least as far as their social life is concerned – then remember that you are doing exactly the same job as these primitive painters, since you provide them with money and sell their canvases, which enables them to produce others.

If a painter ruins himself emotionally by working hard at his painting, and renders himself unfit for so much else, for family life, &c, &c, if, consequently, he paints not only with colour but with self-sacrifice and self-denial and a broken heart, then your own work is not only no better paid, but costs you, in exactly the same way as a painter, this half-deliberate, half-accidental eclipse of your personality.

What I mean is that though you are <u>indirectly</u> involved in painting, you are more productive than I am, for instance. The more completely you are involved in dealing, the more of an artist you become. And so I hope the same thing for myself . . . the more wasted and sick I become, a broken pitcher, the more I may also become a creative artist in this great renaissance of art of which we speak.

All this is certainly so, but eternally continuing art, and this renaissance – this green shoot sprung from the roots of the old sawn-off trunk, these are matters so spiritual that we can't help but feel rather melancholy when we reflect that we could have created life for less than the cost of creating art.

You will be doing well if you can make me feel that art is alive, you who love art perhaps more than I do.

I tell myself that it isn't the fault of art, but my own, that the only means of regaining my confidence and peace of mind is to <u>do better</u>.

And that brings us back again to the end of my last letter – I myself may be getting old, but it would be sheer fantasy to think that art has had its day.

Now, if you know what a 'mousmé' is (you will find out when you read Loti's Madame Chrysanthème), I have just painted one. It took me a whole week, and I haven't been able to do anything else, because I still haven't been too well. That is what annoys me – had I felt well, I would have been able to run off some more landscapes in the meantime, but to do justice to my mousmé I had to conserve my mental energies. A mousmé is a Japanese girl – Provençal in this case – 12 to 14 years old.

That makes 2 figures I've got now, the Zouave and her.

Look after your health, take baths, especially <u>if Gruby has advised you to</u>, for in 4 years' time – which is how much older I am than you – you will realize that reasonably good health is essential for anyone who wants to work. Now, for those of us who work with our brains, our one and only hope of not running out of steam too soon is to prolong our lives artificially by observing an up-to-date health regime as rigorously as we can. I, for one, do not do all I ought to. And a little good humour is worth more than all the medicines in the world.

[. . .]

Bernard has sent me 10 sketches including his brothel. Three of them are in the style of Redon, for whom he feels an enthusiasm I myself do not really share. But there is a woman washing herself, very Rembrandtesque or à la Goya, and a landscape with figures, very strange. He expressly forbade me to send them to you – however you will be receiving them by the same post.

I'm sure Russell will take other things of Bernard's.

I've seen some work by this <u>Boch</u> now, it's strictly impressionist, but not strong, he's still too preoccupied with the new technique to be himself. He will gain in strength and his personality will come out, I think. But MacKnight does watercolours to match those by <u>Destrée</u> – you remember, that revolting Dutchman we used to know. However, he has washed a few small still lifes, a yellow pot on a purple foreground, a red pot on green, an orange pot on blue – better, but still pretty poor.

The village where they are staying is <u>pure Millet</u>, poor peasants, nothing more, absolutely <u>rustic</u> and homely. This feature completely escapes them. I believe that MacKnight has civilized his brute of a landlord, converting him to civilized Christianity. At any rate, this scoundrel and his worthy spouse shake your hand when you go there – it's a café, of course – and when you order a drink they have a way of refusing money, 'Oh, I couldn't take money from an artisst,' with two s's. Anyway, it's their own fault it's so dreadful round there, and this Boch must have become quite stupid in MacKnight's company.

I think MacKnight must have some money, but not much. That's how they contaminate the village. If it weren't for that, I'd go over there quite often to work. What they should not be doing there is passing the time of day with polite society – well, the only people they know are the station master and a score of bores, and that's the main reason why they are getting nowhere. I've already said all this to Mourier, who at one time thought MacKnight had great feeling for 'the man of the soil'.

Naturally, these simple and naïve country folk make fun of them and despise them. Whereas, if they went about their work instead of clinging to these village layabouts with their detachable collars, then they'd be welcome in the peasants' homes and let their owners earn a few coppers. Then this blessed Fontvieille would be a treasure-trove for them, for the natives are – like Zola's humble peasants – innocent and gentle beings, as we know.

No doubt MacKnight will soon be doing little landscapes with sheep, for chocolate boxes.

Not just my pictures but I myself have become especially haggard of late, almost like Hugo van der Goes in the painting by Émile Wauters. Except that, having had all my beard carefully shaved off, I think I'm as much the very placid abbot in that picture as the mad painter so cleverly portrayed in it. And I'm not displeased at falling somewhere between the two, for one must live, especially as there is no getting away from the fact that there may be a crisis one of these days if your situation with the Boussods were to change. All the more reason for keeping up contacts with artists, on my part as much as on yours.

For the rest, I think I have spoken the truth: that I would be doing no more than my duty should I ever manage to pay back in kind the money you have laid out. And <u>in practice</u> that means doing portraits.

As for drinking too much . . . I have no idea if it's a bad thing. Take Bismarck, who, think what you like, is very practical and very intelligent – his good doctor told him that he drank too much and <u>that he'd been putting a severe strain on his stomach and his brain all his life</u>. B. stopped drinking at once. He has gone downhill ever since and is still getting no better. He must be laughing up his sleeve at his doctor, whom, luckily for him, he did not consult sooner.

So there we are. With a hearty handshake,

Ever yours,

Vincent

The portrait of the young girl is on a white background strongly tinged with Veronese green, the bodice is striped blood-red and violet. The skirt is royal blue with large yellow-orange dots. The matt flesh tints are yellowish-grey, the hair purplish-blue, the eyebrows and the eyelashes black, the eyes orange and Prussian blue, & an oleander branch between her fingers, for the 2 hands are in the picture.

Bear in mind that we don't have to change our minds about helping Gauguin if the proposal is acceptable as it is, <u>but we do not need him</u>. So don't think that working by myself worries me and <u>be sure</u> not to press the matter on my account.

520 [F]

[11 August 1888]

My dear Theo,

Before long you will be making the acquaintance of Mr Patience Escalier – a typical 'man of the hoe', a former Camargue herdsman, now a gardener at a farmhouse in the Crau.

I shall be sending you this very day the drawing I did after that painting, just like the drawing I did after the portrait of the postman, Roulin.

The colouring of this peasant portrait isn't as dark as the Nuenen potato eaters, but our so civilized <u>Parisian</u> Portier* – presumably so called because he chucks the

* Doorman

pictures out through the <u>door</u> – will find himself once more faced with the same problem. You have changed since then, but you will find that he has not. It really is a pity that there are not more pictures <u>with clogs</u> in Paris. I don't think my peasant will do any harm, for instance, to your Lautrec, and I even make so bold as to imagine that the Lautrec would appear still more distinguished by the contrast, and that mine would gain by the odd association, because that sunlit, sunburned quality, weatherbeaten by the full sun and open air, would come even more into its own alongside the face powder and the fashionable clothes.

How wrong the Parisians are in not acquiring a taste for things that are out of the ordinary, for Monticellis, for barbotine. Still, one shouldn't be discouraged because Utopia isn't round the corner. It is just that what I learned in Paris <u>is deserting me</u> and that I am going back to the ideas I had in the country before I knew the impressionists. And I shouldn't be very surprised if before very long the impressionists were to find fault with my way of working, which has been enriched by the ideas of Delacroix rather than theirs.

For instead of trying to reproduce exactly what I see before me, I make more arbitrary use of colour to express myself more forcefully. Well, so much for theory, but let me give you an example of what I mean.

I should like to paint the portrait of an artist friend who dreams great dreams, who works as the nightingale sings, because it is his nature. This man will be fair-haired. I should like to put my appreciation, the love

I have for him, into the picture. So I will paint him as he is, as faithfully as I can – to begin with.

But that is not the end of the picture. To finish it, I shall be an obstinate colourist. I shall exaggerate the fairness of the hair, arrive at tones of orange, chrome, pale yellow. Behind the head – instead of painting the ordinary wall of the shabby apartment, I shall paint infinity, I shall do a simple background of the richest, most intense blue that I can contrive, and by this simple combination, the shining fair head against this rich blue background, I shall obtain a mysterious effect, like a star in the deep blue sky.

I used the same approach in the portrait of the peasant. Without wanting in this case, however, to conjure up the mysterious brilliance of a pale star in the blue of infinity. But by imagining the marvellous man that I was about to paint right in the middle of the sweltering midday heat of harvest, I arrived at the flashing orange colours like red-hot iron and the luminous tones of old gold in the shadows.

Ah, my dear brother – and the worthies will see only caricature in this exaggeration. But what does that matter to us? We have read La terre and Germinal, and if we paint a peasant we want to show that what we have read has, in the end, become a small part of us.

I don't know if I can convey the postman <u>as I feel him</u>. This man is a revolutionary like old Tanguy. He is probably considered a good republican, because he heartily detests the republic which we now enjoy, and because all in all he is somewhat doubtful and a little disillusioned with the republican idea itself. But one day I saw him singing the Marseillaise, and I thought I was watching '89, not next year, but the one 99 years ago. It was a Delacroix, a Daumier, straight out of old Holland. Unfortunately he cannot pose, and a painting demands an intelligent model.

I must now tell you that things are extremely grim these days, materially speaking. Whatever I do, life is very expensive here, almost like Paris, where you don't get much for 5 or 6 francs a day.

When I have models, I have to make great sacrifices as a consequence. No matter, I shall continue. And if by chance you should happen to send me a little more money sometimes, I assure you it would benefit the pictures, not me. The only choice I have myself is between being a good painter or a bad one. I choose the first. But the needs of painting are like those of a ruinously expensive mistress, one can do nothing without money, and one never has enough of it. Painting should thus be done at public expense instead of overburdening the artist.

But there, we should keep our own counsel, because <u>no one is forcing us to work</u>, indifference towards painting being inevitably pretty general, pretty well permanent.

Fortunately, my stomach has recovered so much that I have lived 3 weeks of the month on ship's biscuits with milk and eggs. The pleasant heat is restoring my strength. I certainly did the right thing coming south <u>now</u> instead of waiting until my complaint was past curing. Yes, I am as well as other men now, which I have been no more than briefly in the past, in Nuenen for instance – and it is not unpleasant. By 'other men' I mean something like those labourers on strike, or old Tanguy, old Millet, the peasants. When you are in good health you should be able to live on a piece of bread while doing a full day's work and have enough strength left over to smoke and have a drink, <u>because you need that</u> under those conditions. And yet be clearly aware of the stars and infinity on high. Then life seems almost enchanted after all. Ah, those who don't believe in the sun here are quite godless.

Unfortunately, along with the good god sun, there is the devil <u>mistral</u> 3 quarters of the time.

Saturday's post has been, damn it, and I was quite sure that your letter would come, but you can see I'm not getting in a state about it. With a handshake,

Ever yours,
Vincent

534 [F]

[9 September 1888]

My dear Theo,

I have just put the sketch of the new picture, the Night Café, in the post, as well as another that I did some time ago. I might finish by doing a few Japanese prints one day.

Now, yesterday I was busy with the furnishing of the house. Just as the postman & his wife had told me, the two beds will come to 150 fr. each if one wants them to be sturdily made. I found that everything they'd said about prices was true. So I had to change tack, and this is what I've done: I've bought one bed in walnut, and another in deal, which will be mine, and which I shall decorate later. Then I bought bedding for one of the beds, and <u>two</u> mattresses. If Gauguin, or someone else, comes, his bed will be ready in a minute. From the start I wanted to arrange the house, not just for me, but so that I'll be able to put someone up.

Naturally, that swallowed up the greater part of the money. With the rest I bought 12 chairs, a mirror, and a few small necessities. Which means, in short, that I'll be able to move in by next week.

For visitors, there'll be the prettiest room upstairs, which I shall do my best to turn into something like the boudoir of a really artistic woman.

Then there will be my own bedroom, which I want to keep extremely simple, but with large, solid furniture, bed, chairs, table, all in deal.

Downstairs the studio and another room, also a studio, but a kitchen at the same time.

One day you'll see a picture of the little house itself, in bright sunshine, or else with the window lit up and the starry sky.

From now on you can consider yourself the owner of a country house here in Arles. Because I'm very eager to arrange it so that you'll be happy in it, and to turn it into a studio clearly designed as such. If, say, you came for a holiday here in Marseilles in a year's time, it would be ready – and I intend the house to be filled with pictures from top to bottom by then.

The room you'll stay in then, or which will be Gauguin's if Gauguin comes, will have white walls hung with large yellow sunflowers.

In the morning, when you open the window, you'll see the green of the gardens and the rising sun and the road into town.

And you'll see these big pictures of bunches of 12 or 14 sunflowers crammed into this tiny boudoir with its pretty bed and everything else elegantly done. It will be something special.

And the studio – the red tiles on the floor, the walls and ceiling white, the rustic chairs, the deal table – hung, I hope, with portraits. There will be a feeling of Daumier about it – and I'll go so far as to predict that it will be something very special.

Now please would you look out for some Daumier lithographs for the studio, and some Japanese things, but there is absolutely no hurry, and only when you happen to get duplicates of them. And also some Delacroixs, and some ordinary lithographs by modern artists. There is no hurry whatever, but I have it all planned. I really do want to make it – <u>an artist's house</u>, but not affected, on the contrary, <u>nothing affected</u>, but everything from the chairs to the pictures full of character.

As for the beds, I got the sort of beds they have here, large double beds instead of iron bedsteads. They have an air of solidity, permanence and calm, and if that takes a little more bedding, it's too bad, but they must have character. Most luckily, I have a housemaid whom I can rely on, otherwise I shouldn't have dared to start living here. She is quite old and has many varied offspring, and she keeps my tiles nice and red and clean.

I can't tell you how much pleasure it gives me to be tackling such a big and important task. For I hope that what I am doing here will turn out to be one great decoration.

Thus, as I've already told you, I'm going to paint my own bed. There will be 3 subjects on it. Perhaps a nude woman, I haven't decided, perhaps a cradle with a child, I don't know, but I'm going to take my time.

I no longer feel any hesitation at all about staying here, as I have a wealth of ideas for work. I intend to buy something for the house every month now. And given patience, the house will be worth something because of the furniture and the decorations.

I must warn you that very soon I shall be needing a large consignment of paints for the autumn – which I think is going to be absolutely stunning. On second thoughts I am enclosing the order with this.

In my picture of the Night Café, I have tried to express the idea that the café is a place where one can destroy oneself, go mad or commit a crime. In short, I have tried, by contrasting soft pink with blood-red and wine-red, soft Louis XV-green and Veronese green with yellow-greens and harsh blue-greens, all this in an atmosphere of an infernal furnace in pale sulphur, to express the powers of darkness in a common tavern. And yet under an outward show of Japanese gaiety and Tartarin's good nature.

But what would Mr Tersteeg say about this picture, a man who, faced with a Sisley, Sisley mind you, the most unassuming and sensitive of the impressionists, said, 'I can't help thinking that the artist who painted this was a bit tipsy.' Faced with my picture he'd say it was a raging case of delirium tremens.

I can find absolutely nothing to object to in your idea of exhibiting at the Revue Indépendante, provided, that is, I don't make it difficult for those who usually exhibit there.

Except that we must then tell them that I should like to reserve a second exhibition for myself, after this first one, of what are really studies. Then next year I will give them the pictures from the house to exhibit, when the set is complete. Not that I'm all that keen, but I want to make sure that these studies are not taken for compositions, and to convey in advance that the first showing will be one of studies.

For the Sower and the Night Café are the only attempts at finished paintings.

As I write, the poor peasant who resembles a caricature of our father has just come into the café. The resemblance really is striking. Particularly the air of evasiveness and weariness and the vagueness of the mouth. It still seems a pity to me that I haven't been able to do it.

I am adding to this letter the order for paints, which is not exactly urgent, only I am so full of plans, and then autumn promises so many splendid subjects, that I simply don't know if I'll be starting 5 or 10 canvases. It will be just as it was in the spring with the orchards in bloom, the subjects will be endless. If you entrusted old Tanguy with the cruder colour, he would probably make a good job of it.

His other, delicate, colours are really inferior, especially the blues.

I hope to improve the quality a little while preparing the next batch. I am doing relatively less work, and spending longer going back over it. I have kept back 50 francs for the week, the furniture having swallowed up 250 already. Still, I'll be recouping the money. And from today you can tell yourself that you have a kind of country house, unfortunately a little far away. But it would stop being too far away if there were a permanent exhibition in Marseilles. In a year's time that's something we may well see. With a handshake,

Ever yours,
Vincent

539 [F] [PART]

[c. 17 September 1888]

My dear Theo,

I wrote to you earlier this morning, then I went and did some more work on a picture of a sunny garden. Then I brought it back in – and went out again with a blank canvas, and that, too, has been finished. And now I want to write to you again.

You see, I have never had such luck before, nature here is <u>extraordinarily</u> beautiful. Everything and everywhere. The dome of the sky is a wonderful blue, the sun has rays of a pale sulphur, and it is as soft and delightful as the combination of heavenly blues and yellows in Vermeer of Delft. I cannot paint as beautifully, but it absorbs me so much that I let myself go without giving thought to a single rule.

That makes 3 pictures of the gardens opposite my house. Then the two cafés. Then the sunflowers. Then the portrait of Boch and myself. Then the red sun over the factory, and the men unloading sand, and the old mill. Leaving the other studies aside, you can see that there's been some work done.

But my paint, my canvas, my purse, are completely exhausted today. The last picture, done with the last tubes of paint on the last canvas, is of a garden, green by nature, but painted without any actual green, nothing but Prussian blue and chrome yellow. I am beginning to feel completely different from the way I did when I came here. I no longer have doubts, I no longer hesitate to tackle things, and this feeling could well grow.

But what scenery! Where I am there's a public garden right next to the street with the girls of easy virtue, and Mourier, for instance, hardly ever went there even though we go for a walk in the gardens almost every day, on the far side (there are 3 of them). But you see, it's just that which lends a touch of Boccaccio to the place.

That side of the garden, by the way, is for reasons of chastity or morality bare of flowering shrubs such as oleanders. There are ordinary plane trees, groves of stiff pine, a weeping tree and green grass. But it has such intimacy! There are gardens by Manet like that.

For as long as you can bear the burden of all the paint and canvas and all the money that I have to spend, carry on sending it to me, because what I am getting ready will be better than the last batch, and I'm sure we'll make a profit out of it instead of losing, provided I can manage to produce a decent set. Which is what I am trying to do.

But is it absolutely impossible for Thomas to lend me two or three hundred francs against my studies? That would mean I'd earn more than a thousand on them, and I can't tell you how thrilled, thrilled, thrilled I am by what I see. And that fills one with expectations for the autumn, an enthusiasm which makes the time pass without one's feeling it – beware the morning after the night before, and the winter mistrals!

Today, working all the while, I thought a lot about Bernard. His letter is full of veneration for Gauguin's talent – he says that he thinks him so great an artist that he is almost afraid of him, and that he finds everything that he, Bernard, does inadequate in comparison with Gauguin. And you know that last winter Bernard was still picking quarrels with Gauguin. In the long run, be that as it may and whatever happens, it's very comforting that these artists are our friends, and I like to think they'll remain so, no matter how things turn out.

I am so happy with the house – with work – that I even dare to think that this happiness will not remain confined to me, but that you, too, will share in it and have some good luck as well!

Some time ago I read an article on Dante, Petrarch, Boccaccio, Giotto and Botticelli. My God, that made an impression on me, reading the letters of those men! Now Petrarch lived very near here, at Avignon, and I see the same cypresses and oleanders. I have tried to put something of that into one of the Gardens, painted in a thick impasto of lemon yellow and lime green. I was most of all touched by Giotto – <u>always suffering</u>, and always full of benevolence and zeal, as though he were already living in another world.

Giotto is extraordinary, anyway, and I understand him better than I do the poets Dante, Petrarch and Boccaccio. It always seems to me that poetry is more <u>terrible</u> than painting, although painting is dirtier and ultimately more tedious. And the painter on the whole says nothing, he holds his tongue, and I prefer that too.

My dear Theo, when you have seen the cypresses, the oleanders and the sun here – and that day will come, rest assured – then you will think even more often of the beautiful works of Puvis de Chavannes, of Doux pays, and so many others.

There is so much that is Greek throughout both the Tartarin side and the Daumier side of this strange country, where the good people have the accent with which you are familiar, and there is a Venus of Arles just like the Lesbos one, and despite everything, one is still aware of the youth of it all.

I haven't the slightest doubt that one day you too will

know the south. Perhaps you'll go and see Claude Monet when he is in Antibes, or you'll find some opportunity, anyway.

When the mistral blows, however, it is just the opposite of a <u>pleasant</u> country, because the mistral gets on one's nerves badly. But what compensation, what compensation when there is a day without wind. What intensity of colours, what pure air, what vibrant serenity.

Tomorrow I am going to draw until the paint arrives. But I am now resolved not to draw any more pictures with charcoal. It serves no purpose, you must tackle drawings with colour if you want to draw well.

Oh – the exhibition at the Revue Indépendante – good – but once and for all, we have smoked too much to put the wrong end of the cigar in our mouths. We must try to sell if we want to do the things we have sold all over again, but better. It's because we are in a bad trade – but don't let's play to the gallery and suffer for it at home.

This afternoon I had a select audience . . . 4 or 5 pimps and a dozen urchins, who found it extremely interesting watching the paint come out of the tubes. Well, that audience – there's fame for you, or rather, I firmly intend to be as unconcerned about ambition and fame as those urchins and layabouts along the Rhône and the rue du Bout d'Arles.

I went to Milliet's today. He is coming tomorrow, having prolonged his stay by 4 days.

I wish Bernard would do his military service in Africa, because he would do some good things there, and I still don't know what to say to him. He told me that he would exchange his portrait for one of my studies.

But he says he <u>daren't</u> do Gauguin as I asked him to, because he feels too shy in front of Gauguin. Bernard is basically so temperamental!! He can be silly and unpleasant sometimes, but I certainly haven't any right to reproach him, because I myself am only too familiar with that nervous disorder, and I'm sure he would not reproach me either. If he went to Africa to stay with Milliet, Milliet would certainly befriend him, for Milliet is a very loyal friend, and makes love so easily that he almost holds love in contempt.

What is Seurat doing? I wouldn't dare show him the studies I've sent you, but the ones of the sunflowers, and the taverns, and the gardens, I wouldn't mind him seeing those – I often think about his method, and yet I don't follow it at all, but he is an original colourist, and so is Signac, but to a different degree. The pointillists have discovered something new, and anyway I like them a lot. But as far as I am concerned – I tell you frankly – I am going back more to what I was trying to do before I went to Paris, and I don't know if anyone before me has spoken of suggestive colour, but Delacroix and Monticelli did it without talking about it.

But I am the way I was at Nuenen again, when I made a vain effort to learn music – I was keenly aware even then of the relationship between colour and Wagner's music.

Now, it is true that I see in impressionism a resurrection of Eugène Delacroix, but as the interpretations are both divergent and also rather irreconcilable, impressionism cannot yet formulate a doctrine. That is why I am staying with the impressionists, because it means nothing, and commits you to nothing, and as one of them I do not have to take up any position. My God, you have to play the fool in this life. I ask only for time to study, and you, do you ask for anything other than that? I know that you, like me, must love having the peace one needs for objective study.

And I am so afraid of depriving you of it by my demands for money.

And yet, I budget so carefully, but found today again that with the ten metres of canvas I had budgeted accurately for all the colours except one, the fundamental one of yellow. If all my colours are used up at the same time, isn't that proof that I can sense the relative amounts in my sleep? It's the same with drawing, I take hardly any measurements, and in that I differ quite radically from Cormon, who says that if he didn't measure he would draw like a pig.

[. . .]

It's a comfort that we are always engrossed in our raw materials, not speculating but wanting only to produce. And so we cannot go wrong.

I hope it will go on being like that, and if I am doomed to exhaust my paint, my canvas and my purse, not even that will be our undoing, of that you may be sure. Even supposing you exhaust your own purse and everything in it yourself, that would be a serious matter, of course, but just say to me calmly, there is nothing left – and there will still be something left, because of what I have done with your money.

But you will then quite naturally say to me – and in the meantime? In the meantime – I'll do some drawing, since doing nothing but drawing is easier than painting.

A warm handshake. What days these are, not because of what is happening, but because I feel so strongly that you and I are not in decline, nor done for yet, nor are we going to be. But you know, I won't argue with the critics who will say that my pictures are not – finished.

With a handshake, and for now,

Ever yours,
Vincent

I too have read Richepin's Césarine – I very much like what the woman says about that fool: the whole of life is just a matter of the right equations.

[F] [LETTER FROM VINCENT TO PAUL GAUGUIN]

[3 October 1888]

My dear Gauguin,

This morning I received your excellent letter, which I have again sent on to my brother. Your view of impressionism in general, of which your portrait is a symbol, is striking. No one could be more anxious than I am to see it – but I am sure even now that this work is too important for me to take in exchange. But if you would like to keep it for us, my brother will, if you agree, buy it at the first opportunity – and I immediately asked him to do so – so let's hope it happens before long.

For we are trying once more to make it as easy as possible for you to come here soon.

I must tell you that even while working I think continually about the plan of setting up a studio in which you and I will be permanent residents, but which both of us want to turn into a shelter and refuge for friends, against the times when they find that the struggle is getting too much for them.

When you left Paris, my brother and I stayed on together for a time, which will always remain an unforgettable memory for me. The discussions ranged further and wider – with Guillaumin, with the Pissarros, father and son, and with Seurat, whom I had not met before (I visited his studio just a few hours before my departure).

These discussions often dealt with something so near to my brother's heart and to mine, namely what steps to take in order to safeguard the material existence of painters, to safeguard their means of production (paints, canvases) and to safeguard their true share in the price their pictures fetch these days – though not until long after they have left the artists' possession.

When you're here, we can mull over all these discussions.

Anyway, when I left Paris I was in a sorry state, quite ill and almost an alcoholic after driving myself on even while my strength was failing – and then withdrawing into myself, still bereft of hope.

Now, hope is vaguely beckoning on the horizon again, that flickering hope which used sometimes to console my solitary life.

I should so much like to imbue you with a large share of my faith that we shall succeed in starting something that will endure.

When we have had a talk about those strange days spent in discussion in run-down studios and the cafés of the Petit Boulevard, you will understand the full scope of this idea of my brother's and mine – as yet unrealized when it comes to setting up a society.

Still, you will appreciate that in order to remedy the terrible situation of the last few years something is needed, either along the precise lines we proposed or else very much like them. That much we have taken for our unshakeable foundation, as you will gather when you have the full explanation. And you will agree that we have gone a <u>good way beyond</u> the plan we have already communicated to you. That we have gone beyond it is no more than our duty as picture dealers, for you probably know that I, too, spent several years in the trade and do not despise a profession in which I used to earn my living. Suffice it to say that I'm sure that, although you have apparently cut yourself off from Paris, you haven't stopped feeling a fairly close rapport with Paris.

I am having an extraordinary spell of feverish activity these days. Right now I am tackling a landscape with a blue sky above an immense green, purple and yellow vineyard, with black and orange vines. Little figures of ladies with red parasols and little figures of grape pickers with their small cart make it even gayer. Grey sand in the foreground. Another size 30 square canvas to decorate the house.

I've a portrait of myself, all ash grey. The ashen colour – which has been obtained by mixing Veronese green with orange lead – on a pale Veronese background, all in harmony with the reddish-brown clothes. Not wishing to inflate my own personality, however, I aimed rather for the character of a bonze, a simple worshipper of the eternal Buddha. Though I have taken rather a lot of trouble with it, I shall have to go over it again if I want to express the idea properly, and I shall have to recover even further from the stultifying effect of our so-called state of civilization if I am to have a better model for a better picture.

One thing that gives me enormous pleasure is the letter I received yesterday from Boch (his sister is one of the Belgian Vingtistes), who writes that he has settled down in the Borinage to paint miners and coal mines there. He nevertheless intends to return to the south – to vary his impressions – and if he does he is certain to come to Arles.

I consider my views of art excessively run of the mill compared with yours.

I have always had coarse animal tastes.

I neglect everything for the external beauty of things, which I cannot reproduce because I render it so ugly and coarse in my pictures, albeit nature seems so perfect to me.

At present, however, my bony carcass is so full of energy that it makes straight for its objective. The result is a degree of sincerity, perhaps original at times, about what I feel, but only if the subject lends itself to my crude and clumsy touch.

I feel sure that if from now on you were to consider yourself the head of this studio, which we shall try to ensure will become a refuge for many – little by little, as our unremitting labour provides us with the means of completing it – I'm sure that you would then feel more or less consoled for the present ordeals of penury and ill-health, seeing that we shall probably be devoting our lives to a generation of painters that will last a long while to come.

This part of the country has already seen the cult of Venus – in Greece, primarily artistic – followed by the poets and artists of the Renaissance. Where these things could flourish, impressionism can as well.

I have made a special decoration, the <u>Poet's Garden</u>, for the room you will have (there is a first draft of it among the sketches in Bernard's possession – it was later simplified). The ordinary public garden contains plants and shrubs that conjure up landscapes in which one can readily imagine Botticelli, Giotto, Petrarch, Dante and Boccaccio. I have tried to distil in the decoration the essence of what constitutes the immutable character of this country.

And I set out to paint that garden in such a way that one is put in mind of the old poet from these parts (or rather from Avignon), Petrarch, and of the new poet from these parts – Paul Gauguin –

However clumsy this attempt may be, it may show you perhaps that I have been thinking of you with very great emotion as I prepared your studio.

Let us be of good heart about the success of our venture, and please keep thinking of this as your home, for I feel very sure that all this will last for a very long time.

A warm handshake, and believe me,

Ever yours,
Vincent

I am only afraid that you will think Brittany more beautiful, indeed, that you will find nothing more beautiful here than Daumier, the figures here are often pure Daumier. It shouldn't take you long to discover that antiquity and the Renaissance lie dormant under all this modernity. Well, you are free to revive them.

Bernard tells me that he, Morel, Laval and somebody else will be making exchanges with me. In principle I am very much in favour of the system of exchanges between artists because I have seen the important part it played in the life of the Japanese painters. Accordingly, one of these days I shall be sending you what studies I have that are dry and that I can spare, so that you may have first pick. But I shall make no exchanges at all with you if it means that on your side it costs you something as important as your portrait, which is sure to be too beautiful. Truly, I wouldn't dare, because my brother would gladly buy it from you for a whole month's money.

554 [F]

[16 October 1888]

My dear Theo,

I'm sending you a little sketch at long last to give you at least some idea of the direction my work is taking. Because I feel quite well again today. My eyes are still tired, but I had a new idea all the same and here is the sketch of it.

As always a size 30 canvas.

This time it's simply my bedroom. Only here everything depends on the colour, and by simplifying it I am lending it more style, creating an overall impression <u>of rest or sleep</u>. In fact, a look at the picture ought to rest the mind, or rather the imagination.

The walls are pale violet. The floor – is red tiles.

The wood of the bed and the chairs is the yellow of fresh butter, the sheet and the pillows very light lime green.

The blanket scarlet.

The window green.

The washstand orange, the basin blue.

The doors lilac.

And that's all – nothing of any consequence in this shuttered room.

The sturdy lines of the furniture should also express undisturbed rest.

Portraits on the wall, and a mirror, and a hand towel, and some clothes. The frame – because there is no white in the picture – will be white.

This by way of revenge for the enforced rest I have had to take.

I shall work on it again all day tomorrow, but you can see how simple the conception is. The shadows and the cast shadows are left out and it is painted in bright flat tints like the Japanese prints.

It will form a contrast to, for example, the Tarascon diligence and the Night Café.

I am not writing you a long letter because I intend starting very early tomorrow in the cool morning light so as to finish my canvas.

How are your aches and pains? Don't forget to let me know.

I hope you'll write one of these days.

One day I'll do some sketches for you of the other rooms too.

With a good handshake,

Ever yours,
Vincent

557 [F]

[24 October 1888]

My dear Theo,

Thanks for your letter and the 50 fr. note. As you learned from my telegram, Gauguin has arrived in good health. He even seems to be in better health than I am.

He is very happy about the sale you made, of course, and I no less so, since some still absolutely essential settling-in expenses will now no longer need to wait, nor will you be saddled with all of them. G. will undoubtedly be writing to you today.

He is very, very interesting as a man, and I have every confidence that we shall achieve a great deal with him. He will undoubtedly be very productive here, and I hope that I may be, too.

And so I dare hope the burden will be <u>a little</u> less heavy for you, I even hope <u>much</u> less heavy.

I realize, to the point of being morally crushed and physically drained by it, that taking all in all, I have absolutely no other means of ever recovering what we have spent.

I cannot help it that my pictures do not sell.

The day will come, however, when people will see they are worth more than the price of the paint and my living expenses, very meagre on the whole, which we put into them.

As far as money or finances are concerned, what I want and what I am interested in is to have no debts in the first place.

But, my dear brother, my debt is so great that by the time I have paid it off, which I'm still sure I'll succeed in doing, the strain of producing pictures will have taken my whole life, and it will seem to me that I haven't lived. The only thing is that producing pictures may become a little more difficult for me, and that, in time, there won't always be so many.

That they are not selling at the moment distresses me because you suffer for it, but if my bringing nothing in did not inconvenience you, it wouldn't matter much either way to me.

But as far as finances are concerned, all I need is to remember this truth, that a man who lives for 50 years and spends two thousand a year, spends a hundred thousand francs, and that he must therefore also bring in a hundred thousand. To do a thousand pictures at a hundred francs during one's lifetime as an artist is a very, very, very difficult thing to do, and since the pictures do indeed fetch a hundred francs . . . then . . . our task is very hard at times. But there is nothing we can do to change that.

We shall probably give Tasset a miss altogether, because we are going – to a large extent – to make use of cheaper paints, Gauguin as well as I. As for the canvas, we shall prepare it ourselves for the same reason.

I had the feeling for a time that I was going to be ill, but Gauguin's arrival has so taken my mind off it that

I am sure it will pass. I must pay attention to my diet for a while, but that's all – absolutely nothing else. And before very long you will have some work.

Gauguin has brought a magnificent canvas which he'd exchanged with Bernard, Breton women in a green field, white, black, green, and a note of red, and matt flesh tones. So, let's all be of good heart.

I'm sure the day will come when I shall sell as well, but I am so far behind with you, and am still spending without bringing anything in. From time to time that thought saddens me.

I am very, very pleased with what you write about one of the Dutchmen coming to stay with you, so that you too will no longer be alone. It's very, very good news, especially since winter will soon be here.

Anyway, I'm in a hurry now, and must go out and start work again on another size thirty canvas.

Soon, when Gauguin writes to you, I'll add another letter to his.

Of course, I don't know in advance what Gauguin will say about this part of the world, and about our life, but he's very pleased at any rate about the good sale you made for him.

Goodbye for the present, and a good handshake,

Ever yours,
Vincent

564 [F]

[second half of December 1888]

My dear Theo,

Yesterday Gauguin and I went to Montpellier to see the gallery there, particularly the Bruyas room, where there are lots of portraits of Bruyas by Delacroix, Ricard, Courbet, Cabanel, Couture, Verdier, Tassaert and others. There are also other paintings by Delacroix, Courbet, Giotto, Paulus Potter, Botticelli, Th. Rousseau, very fine.

Bruyas was a benefactor of artists, and I shall say no more to you than that. In the portrait by Delacroix he is a gentleman with a beard and red hair, who bears an amazing resemblance to you and to me, and made me think of that poem by Musset: Partout où j'ai touché la terre – un malheureux vêtu de noir auprès de nous venait s'asseoir qui nous regardait comme un frère.[*] It would have the same effect on you, I'm sure.

Do go to that bookshop where they sell lithographs of past and present artists, and try, if it doesn't cost too much, to get the lithograph after Delacroix's Le Tasse dans la prison des fous, since I think that figure

---

[*] 'Whenever I touched the earth, a poor wretch dressed in black came and sat down next to us and looked at us like a brother' (misquote from Alfred de Musset, 'Le nuit de Décembre').

must have some connection with this fine portrait of Bruyas.

There are other Delacroixs there, a study of a mulatto woman (which Gauguin copied at one time), Les odalisques, Daniel dans la fosse aux lions, and, by Courbet, I. Les demoiselles de village, magnificent, a nude woman viewed from behind, another lying on the ground in a landscape, La fileuse (superb), and lots of other Courbets. Anyway, you must know of the existence of this collection, or at least know people who have seen it, and who can talk about it. So I will not dwell on the gallery (except on the Barye drawings and bronzes!).

Gauguin and I discuss Delacroix, Rembrandt, etc., a great deal. The debate is <u>exceedingly electric</u>, and sometimes when we finish our minds are as drained as an electric battery after discharge.

We had been right in the midst of magic, for as Fromentin puts it so well: Rembrandt is above all a magician and Delacroix is a man of God, a fantastic man of God, and that's bloody well all there is to it in the name of God.

I am writing you this in connection with our Dutch friends, De Haan and Isaäcson, who have studied and admired Rembrandt so much, hoping that you will encourage them to continue their research.

There must be no discouragement when it comes to that.

You know the strange and superb portrait of a man by

Rembrandt in the Lacaze Gallery? I said to Gauguin that I saw a certain family or racial resemblance to Delacroix or to Gauguin himself in it.

I don't know why, but I always call this portrait 'the traveller' or the man come from afar.

It's a similar and parallel idea to the one I've mentioned to you, to see your future self in the portrait of the old Six, that fine portrait with the gloves, and your past and present in Rembrandt's etching entitled Six reading near a window in a ray of sunshine.

So that's where we've got to.

Gauguin said to me this morning, when I asked him how he was, 'that he felt his former self coming back', which gave me great pleasure. When I came here last winter, weary and almost mentally exhausted, I had to suffer a little inwardly too before I could start on my recovery.

How I wish that you could see the gallery in Montpellier some time, there are some very beautiful things there!

Tell Degas that Gauguin and I have been to see the portrait of Bruyas by Delacroix at Montpellier. Because we must dare to believe that what is, is, and the portrait of Bruyas by Delacroix resembles you and me like another brother.

As far as founding an artists' colony for friends is concerned, such strange things have been known, and I'll close with what you're always saying – only time will tell. You can say all that to our friends Isaäcson and De Haan, and even feel free to read this letter to them. I would have written to them already if I had felt the necessary electric charge.

A very hearty handshake to you all on behalf of Gauguin as well as me.

Ever yours,
Vincent

In case you think that Gauguin or I get down to work effortlessly, let me tell you that work does not always come easily to us. And my wish for our Dutch friends, and for you as well, is that they should feel no more discouraged by their difficulties than we do.

565 [F]

[23 December 1888]

My dear Theo,

Thank you very much for your letter, for the 100 fr. note enclosed and also for the money order for 50 fr.

I think that Gauguin was a little disenchanted with the good town of Arles, the little yellow house where we work, and above all with me.

Indeed, there are serious problems to overcome here still, for him as well as for me.

But these problems lie more in ourselves than anywhere else.

In short, I think that he'll either simply leave or he'll simply stay.

I've told him to think it over and weigh up the pros and cons before doing anything.

Gauguin is very strong, very creative, but he needs peace precisely because of that.

Will he find it elsewhere if he doesn't find it here?

I await his decision with absolute equanimity.

With a good handshake,

Vincent

III

Towards the End

Arles

On 23rd December 1888, van Gogh's strained relationship with Gaugin had come to a head, with van Gogh threatening his friend with a razor. The following morning, van Gogh was found by police unconscious in his bed, having cut a piece from his earlobe. He was admitted to the local hospital, where he was treated by Dr Félix Rey.

570 [F] [part]

[9 January 1889]

My dear Theo,

[. . .]

Physically I am well. The wound is healing very well, and the great loss of blood is righting itself, as I am eating well and my digestion is good. The thing I <u>dread</u> most is insomnia, but the doctor hasn't mentioned it to me, nor have I mentioned it to him as yet. But I am fighting that myself.

I fight it with a very, very strong dose of camphor in my pillow and my mattress, and if ever you're unable to sleep, I recommend this to you. I very much dreaded the idea of sleeping alone in the house, and I've been worried about not being able to fall asleep, but all that's quite over now and I dare say it won't recur.

In hospital I suffered terribly from it, and yet during it all, when it was worse than losing consciousness, I can tell you as an odd fact that I continued to think about Degas. Gauguin and I had been talking about Degas beforehand, and I had pointed out to Gauguin that Degas had said . . . 'I am saving myself for the Arlesiennes.'

Now you know how discerning Degas is, so on your return to Paris, just tell Degas that I confess that up to now I have been powerless to paint the women of Arles without venom, and that he mustn't believe Gauguin if Gauguin is too quick to speak well of my work, since it is nothing more than that of a sick man.

Now if I recover, I <u>must start afresh</u>, but I shall never again be able to reach the heights to which the illness to some extent led me.

[. . .]

Ever yours,
Vincent

[F] [LETTER FROM VINCENT TO PAUL GAUGUIN]

[c. 22 January 1889]

My dear friend Gauguin,

Thank you for your letter. Left behind alone on board my little yellow house – as it was perhaps my duty anyway to be the last to leave – I am not a little put out at my friends' departure.

Roulin got his transfer to Marseilles and has just left. It has been touching to see him these last few days with little Marcelle, making her laugh and dandling her on his knee.

His transfer means his being separated from his family, and you will not be surprised that the one you and I nicknamed 'the passer-by' one evening, was very heavy-hearted. As was I, witnessing that and other upsetting things.

When he sang to his child, his voice took on a strange timbre in which one could hear the voice of a woman rocking a cradle or of a sorrowing wet-nurse, and then another trumpet sound like a clarion call to France.

I reproach myself now that it was I – perhaps insisting too much that you stay on here to await events and giving you so many good reasons for doing so – I reproach myself now that it was I who was perhaps the cause of your departure – unless, of course, that departure was planned beforehand? And that it was therefore perhaps up to me to show I still had the right to be kept fully in the picture.

Be that as it may, I hope we still like each other enough to be able, if need be, to start afresh, assuming that the wolf at the door, alas ever-present for those of us artists without means, should necessitate such a measure.

You mention a canvas of mine in your letter – Sunflowers on a yellow background – and make it plain you'd rather like to have it. I don't think it's altogether a bad choice – for if Jeannin can claim the peony, and Quost the hollyhock, then surely I, above all others, can lay claim to the sunflower.

I think I'll begin by returning what is yours, while observing that it is my intention, after what has happened, categorically to deny your right to the canvas in question. But since I commend your intelligence in choosing this canvas, I'll make the effort to paint two of them exactly alike. In which case it can all be done and settled amicably so that you can have your own in the end all the same.

I made a fresh start today on my canvas of Mme Roulin, the one in which, due to my accident, the hands had been left unfinished. As an arrangement of colours, the reds moving through to pure orange, building up again in the flesh tones to the chromes, passing through the pinks and blending with the olive and Veronese greens – as an impressionist arrangement of colours I have never devised anything better. And I'm sure that if one were to put this canvas just as it is in a fishing boat, even one from Iceland, there would be some among the fishermen who would feel they were there, inside the cradle.

Ah! My dear friend, to achieve in painting what the music of Berlioz and Wagner has already done . . . an art that offers consolation for the broken-hearted! There are still just a few who feel it as you and I do!!!

My brother understands you well and when he tells me that you are a poor sort of wretch like me, well, that just proves that he understands us.

I shall send you your things, but I still have bouts of weakness at times during which I'm in no position to lift even a finger to return your things to you. In a few days' time I'll pluck up the courage. And as for the 'fencing masks and gloves' (make as little use as possible of less infantile engines of war), these terrible engines of war will just have to wait until then. I am writing to you very calmly, but packing up what's left is still beyond me.

In my mental or nervous fever, or madness – I am not too sure how to put it or what to call it – my thoughts sailed over many seas. I even dreamed of the phantom Dutch ship and of Le Horla, and it seems that, while thinking what the woman rocking the cradle sang to rock the sailors to sleep, I, who on other occasions cannot even sing a note, came out with an old nursery tune, something I had tried to express in an arrangement of colours before I fell ill, because I don't know the music of Berlioz.

It would give me great pleasure if you would write to me again soon. Have you finished reading all of Tartarin? The imagination of the south makes for friendship, believe me, and the two of us will always be friends.

Have you read and re-read Uncle Tom's Cabin by Beecher Stowe yet? Perhaps it's not very well written from a literary point of view. Have you read Germinie Lacerteux yet?

With a whole-hearted handshake,

Ever yours,

Vincent

588 [F]

[30 April 1889]

My dear Theo,

On the occasion of the first of May I wish you a tolerably good year, and above all good health.

How I should like to pass on to you some of my physical strength, I have the feeling I've too much of it at the moment. Which does not prevent my head from still not being all that it should be.

How right Delacroix was, who lived on bread and wine alone, and who succeeded in finding a way of life in keeping with his vocation. But the inevitable question of money is ever-present – Delacroix had private means. Corot too. And Millet – Millet was a peasant and the son of a peasant.

You may perhaps be interested in reading this article I cut out of a Marseilles paper because one catches a glimpse of Monticelli in it, and I find the description of the painting representing a corner of the churchyard very interesting. But alas, it's yet another deplorable story.

How sad it is to think that a painter who succeeds, even if only in part, pulls along half a dozen artists who are worse failures than himself.

However, remember Pangloss, remember Bouvard et Pécuchet – I do – and even that becomes clear then. But perhaps those people don't know Pangloss, or else, fatally marked by real despair and great suffering, they have forgotten all they knew about him.

And anyway, we are falling back again in the name of optimism on a religion that strikes me as the rear end of some sort of Buddhism. No harm in that, on the contrary, if that's what one wants.

I don't like the article on Monet in the Figaro very much – how much better that other article in the 19me Siècle was! One could see the pictures in that, and this one is full of nothing but depressing banalities.

Today I am in the middle of packing a case of pictures and studies. I've stuck some newspapers on to one which is flaking – it's one of the best, and I think that when you've had a look at it you'll understand more clearly what my studio, now come to grief, could have been. This study, just like some of the others, was spoiled by the damp while I was ill.

The flood water came up to within a stone's throw of the house, and more important, since the house wasn't heated during my absence, by the time I got back water and saltpetre were oozing from the walls.

That was a blow for me, since not only the studio had come to grief, but even the studies that would have been reminders of it. It is all so final, and my urge to found something very simple but lasting was so strong. I was fighting a losing battle, or rather it was weakness of character on my part, for I am left with feelings of deep remorse about it, difficult to describe. I think that was the reason I cried out so much during the attacks – I wanted to defend myself and couldn't do it. For it was not to me, it was precisely to painters such as the poor wretch about whom the enclosed article speaks that the studio could have been of use.

In fact, we had several predecessors. Bruyas at Montpellier gave a whole fortune to that, a whole life, and without the slightest apparent result.

Yes – a chilly room in the municipal gallery where you can see a troubled face and many fine pictures, where you certainly feel moved, but, alas, moved as in a graveyard.

Yet it would be difficult to walk through a graveyard that demonstrated more clearly the existence of that Espérance which Puvis de Chavannes has painted.

Pictures fade like flowers – even some of Delacroix's have suffered in this way, the magnificent Daniel, Les odalisques (quite different from those in the Louvre, it was in a single range of purplish-blue), but how they impressed me, those pictures fading there, little understood, that's for sure, by most of the visitors who look at Courbet and Cabanel and Victor Giraud, &c.

What are we, we other painters?

Oh, well, I'm sure Richepin is quite right, for instance when he brutally bursts in and consigns them straight back to the madhouse with his profanities.

However, I assure you that I know of no hospital where they would be willing to take me in for nothing, even supposing that I myself shouldered the painting expenses and left the whole of my work to the hospital.

And that is, I don't say a great, but still a small injustice. Even so, I should feel resigned if one took me in. If I were without your friendship, they would drive me remorselessly to suicide, and coward that I am, I should end by committing it. At this point, I hope, we are permitted to protest against society and to defend ourselves.

You can be fairly sure that the Marseilles artist who committed suicide in no way did it under the influence of absinthe, for the simple reason that no one is likely to have offered him any and he could not have had anything to buy it with. Besides, he would not have drunk it purely for pleasure, but because, being ill already, he kept himself going with it.

M. Salles has been to Saint-Rémy – they are not willing to give me permission to paint outside the institution, nor to take me for less than 100 francs.

So this is pretty bad news.

If I could get out of this mess by joining the Foreign Legion for 5 years, I think I should prefer that.

For on the one hand, being locked up and not working, I should find it hard to get better, and on the other hand, they would make us pay 100 francs a month during the whole long life of a madman.

It's a bad business, and what are we to make of it? But would they be willing to have me as a soldier?

I feel very tired after the conversation with M. Salles, and I don't quite know what to do. I myself advised Bernard to do his service there, so it's hardly surprising that I'm considering going to Arabia as a soldier myself.

I say that so you will not blame me too much if I do go. Everything else is so vague and so strange. And you know how doubtful it is that one will ever get back what it costs to paint. For the rest, it seems I am physically well.

Supposing I am only allowed to work under supervision! And in the institution – my God, is it worth paying money for that? In that case I could certainly work just as well, even better, in the barracks.

Anyway, I'm thinking about it. You do so as well. Let us remember that all is for the best in the best of all worlds – it's not impossible.

A really good handshake,

Ever yours,
Vincent

Here is what I think is worth putting on stretchers from the consignment:

The Night Café	– The Alyscamps (lane of tombs)
The Green Vineyard	– ditto
The Red Vineyard	– Garden with large conifer
	bush and oleanders
The Bedroom	
The Furrows	– ditto with cedar & geraniums
	ditto
	– Sunflowers
Portrait of Boch	Flowers, scabious, &c.
" " Laval	ditto, asters, marigolds, &c.
" " Gauguin	
" " Bernard	

The packing case contains some studies by Gauguin which belong to him, and his two fencing masks and some fencing gloves.

If there is room in the packing case, I'll add some stretchers.

Saint-Rémy

592 [F] [part]

[22 May 1889]

My dear Theo,

[. . .] Here is a new size 30 canvas, again as run of the mill as a cheap chromo, depicting age-old love nests in the greenery. Large tree trunks covered with ivy, the ground similarly covered with ivy & periwinkle, a stone bench and a bush of roses, pale in the cool shadow. In the foreground, some plants with white calyxes. It is green, violet and pink.

It's all a question – and this is unfortunately missing from the cheap chromos as well as from the barrel organs – of putting some style into it.

Since I've been here, there's been enough work for me to do, what with the neglected garden with its tall pines and long, unkempt grass mixed with all sorts of weeds, and I haven't even been outside.

However, the countryside around St Rémy is very

beautiful, and little by little I shall probably make a few short trips.

But while I stay here, the doctor is of course in a better position to see what is wrong, & will have his mind set at rest, I hope, about what he can let me paint.

I assure you that I am all right here, and that for the time being I see no reason at all to take lodgings in or around Paris. I have a small room with greenish-grey paper and two sea-green curtains with a design of very pale roses, brightened with touches of blood red.

These curtains, probably the legacy of some deceased and ruined rich person, are very pretty in design. A very worn armchair, probably from the same source, is covered with a tapestry speckled like a Diaz or a Monticelli in brown, red, pink, white, cream, black, forget-me-not blue and bottle green. Through the iron-barred window I can see an enclosed square of wheat, a prospect like a Van Goyen, above which, in the morning, I watch the sun rise in all its glory.

In addition – as there are more than 30 empty rooms – I have another room for doing my work.

The food is all right as far as it goes. It tastes a bit musty, of course, as in a cockroach-infested restaurant in Paris, or in a boarding house. The poor wretches here, having absolutely nothing to do (not a book, nothing more to distract them than a game of boules or a game of draughts), have no other daily distraction than to stuff themselves with chick peas, haricot beans, lentils and other groceries and colonial produce, in set amounts and at stated hours.

As the digestion of these foodstuffs offers certain

difficulties, they fill their days in a manner as inoffensive as it is costly.

But joking apart, my fear of madness is wearing off markedly, since I can see at close quarters those who are affected by it in the same way as I may very easily be in the future.

Previously, I was repelled by these individuals, and I found it distressing to have to reflect that so many in our trade, Troyon, Marchal, Méryon, Jundt, M. Maris, Monticelli, and a whole lot more finished up like that. It was quite impossible for me to picture them in that condition.

Well, now I can think of all that without fear, that's to say, I find it no more dreadful than if those people had died of something else, consumption or syphilis, for example. I see these artists being reinvested with their old serenity, and don't you think it's quite something to meet these old colleagues of ours again? That, joking apart, is what I am profoundly thankful for.

For though there are some who howl or rave a great deal, there is <u>much</u> true friendship here. They say we must tolerate others so that the others may tolerate us, and other very sound arguments, which they put into practice, too. And we understand each other very well. Sometimes, for instance, I can talk with one of them – who can only reply in incoherent sounds – because he is not afraid of me.

[. . .]

You could take the canvases at Tanguy's or at your place off the stretchers, if they're dry enough, and then put on any new ones you think are worth it.

Gauguin ought to be able to tell you the address of

someone who could reline the Bedroom and who won't be too expensive. The restoration ought, I <u>imagine</u>, to cost 5 francs. If it is more, then don't have it done. I'm sure Gauguin didn't pay any more on the many occasions when he had his canvases, or Cezanne's, or Pissarro's, relined.

Again – speaking of my condition – I am so grateful for yet another thing. I've noticed that others, too, hear sounds and strange voices during their attacks, as I did, and that things seemed to change before their very eyes. And that lessened the horror with which I remembered my first attack, something that, when it comes upon you unexpectedly, cannot but frighten you terribly. Once you know it is part of the illness, you accept it like anything else. Had I not seen other lunatics close to, I should not have been able to stop myself from thinking about it all the time. For the suffering and the anguish are not funny when you are having an attack.

Most epileptics bite their tongues and injure them-selves. Rey told me that he had seen a case who had injured his ear, just as I did, and I think I heard a doctor from here, who came to see me with the director, say that he too had seen it before. I like to think that once you know what it is, once you are conscious of your con-dition, and of being subject to attacks, then you can do something to prevent your being taken unawares by the anguish or the terror. Now that it has all been abating for 5 months I have high hopes of getting over it, or at least of no longer having such violent attacks.

There is someone here who has been shouting and

talking like me <u>all the time</u> for a fortnight. He thinks he hears voices and words in the echo of the corridors, probably because his auditory nerve is diseased and over-sensitive, and in my case it was both sight and hearing at the same time, which is usual at the outset of epilepsy, according to what Rey said one day.

Now, the shock was such that even moving made me feel sick, and nothing would have pleased me more than never to have woken up again. At present this <u>horror of life</u> is already less pronounced, and the melancholy less acute. But I still have no <u>will</u>, and hardly any desires, or none at all that are to do with ordinary life, for example, almost no wish to see friends, although I do think of them. That is why I am still not ready to leave here now or in the near future. I should feel depressed about everything again.

And anyway, it is only recently that my loathing of life has been drastically changed. There is still a long way to go from that to willing and doing.

What a pity that you're condemned to stay full-time in Paris and that you never see any part of the country-side other than that around Paris. I'm sure it's no worse for me to be in the company I now find myself than for you to be with that ill-fated Goupil & Cie all the time. In that respect, we are pretty equal. For you, too, are only able to act partly in keeping with your ideas. However, once we've got used to these difficulties, it all becomes second nature.

Although the pictures swallow up canvas and paint, &c, nevertheless at the end of the month I'm sure it's more profitable to spend a little more on those, making use of what I've learned, than to abandon it all, when you have to pay for my board and lodging anyway. And that's why I'm carrying on. So this month I have 4 size 30 canvases and two or three drawings.

But the question of money, whatever one does, is always with us, like the enemy facing the troops, and cannot be denied or ignored.

As much as anyone, I know where my duties lie in that respect. And I may yet be able to pay back everything I've spent, for I consider it to have been, if not taken from you, at least taken from the family. So that's why I've been producing pictures and shall be doing some more. This is acting as you yourself are acting. If I were a man of means, perhaps my mind would be freer to produce art for art's sake. Now I content myself with the thought that by working diligently, one may perhaps make some progress even without thinking about it.

Here are the paints I need:

> 3 emerald green
> 2 cobalt
> 1 ultramarine   large tubes
> 1 orange lead
> 6 zinc white
> 5 metres of canvas

Thanking you for your kind letter, I shake your hand warmly, as I do your wife's.

Ever yours,
Vincent

604 [F] [PART]

[5 or 6 September 1889]

My dear brother,

I have already written to you, but there are still quite a few things you said to me that I haven't answered yet. Firstly, that you have rented a room in Tanguy's house & that my canvases are there, which is very interesting – provided you aren't paying too much – the expenses go on all the time and the canvases still take so long to bring anything in – it often frightens me.

Be that as it may, I'm sure it's a very good step, and I thank you for taking it, as for so many other things. It is curious that Maus had the idea of inviting young Bernard & me for the next Vingtistes exhibition. I should like to exhibit with them very much, though I'm conscious of my inferiority by the side of so many tremendously talented Belgians.

This Mellery, now, is a great artist. And has been one for a number of years. But I shall try my best to do something good this autumn.

I am working away in my room without interruption which does me good and chases away what I imagine are abnormal ideas.

Thus I've done the canvas of the Bedroom again. That's certainly one of my best studies – and sooner or later it must definitely be <u>relined</u>. It was painted so quickly and has dried in such a way that the turpentine evaporated straight away and the paint hasn't stuck firmly to the canvas at all. That will also have happened with other studies of mine painted very quickly and with a very full brush. Anyway, after some time this thin canvas deteriorates and cannot take a lot of impasto. You've got some excellent stretchers, damn it, if I had some like that to work with, I'd be a lot better off than with these battens you get here which warp in the sun.

They say – and I am very willing to believe it – that it is difficult to know oneself – but it isn't easy to paint oneself either. So I am working on two self-portraits at the moment – for want of another model.

Because it is high time that I did a little figure work. In the one I began the first day I got up, I was thin and deathly pale. It is dark purple-blue, and the head whitish with yellow hair, thus with a colour effect.

But I have since started another, three-quarter length on a light background.

Then I'm retouching this summer's studies – in fact, I am working morning, noon and night.

Are you well? – damn it, I really wish that you were 2 years further on and that these early days of marriage, however lovely they may be at times, were behind you. I'm quite convinced that a marriage grows better with time and that it's <u>then</u> that your constitution improves.

So take things with a pinch of northern phlegm, and look after yourselves, both of you. This confounded life in the art world is exhausting, it seems.

Day by day my own strength is returning, and already

I feel I have almost too much of it again. For one doesn't need to be Hercules to remain hard at work at the easel.

What you told me about Maus having been to see my canvases made me think a lot about the Belgian painters these last few days and also during my illness. As a result I was overwhelmed with memories as by an avalanche, and I tried to recall the whole of that school of modern Flemish artists until I felt as homesick as a fish out of water.

Which isn't any good, as our way lies – forwards – and retracing our steps is both impossible and impermissible. In other words one can think about the past without being swamped by an over-melancholic nostalgia.

Anyway, Henri Conscience may not be a perfect writer by any means, but no two ways about it, what a painter! And what loving-kindness in what he said and hoped for. There's a preface in one of his books on my mind all the time (the one to Le conscrit), where he writes that he has been very ill, and says that during his illness, despite all his efforts, he felt his affection for mankind draining away, but that his feelings of love returned on long walks in the countryside.

The inevitability of suffering and despair – well, here I am, bucked up again for a time – and I thank him for it.

I am writing you this letter bit by bit in the intervals when I am worn out with painting. The work is going fairly well. I'm struggling with a canvas I started a few days before my illness – a reaper. The study is all yellow, extremely thickly painted, but the subject was beautiful and simple. For I see in this reaper – a vague figure toiling away for all he's worth in the midst of the heat to finish his task – I see in him the image of death, in the sense that humanity might be the wheat he is reaping. So it is, if you like, the opposite of the sower which I tried to do before. But there is no sadness in this death, this one takes place in broad daylight with a sun flooding everything with a light of pure gold.

Well, here I am, at it again. But I won't give in, and shall try once more on a new canvas. Ah, I could almost believe that I have a new spell of lucidity before me.

So what next – carrying on here for the next few months, or moving elsewhere – I don't know. It's just that the attacks, when they come, are no joke, and running the risk of having a bout like that at your place or at anyone else's is a serious matter.

My dear brother – I always write to you in between bouts of work, & I am working like one truly possessed, more than ever I am in the grip of a pent-up fury of work, and I'm sure it will help to cure me. Perhaps something along the lines of what Eug. Delacroix spoke of will happen to me – 'I discovered painting when I had neither teeth nor breath left,' in the sense that my sad illness makes me work in a pent-up fury – very slowly – but without leaving off from morning till night – and – that is probably the secret – to work long and slowly. But what do I know about it? Still, I think I've one or two canvases on the go which are not too bad, firstly, the reaper in the yellow wheat, and the portrait on a light background which should go to the

Vingtistes, if indeed they remember me when the time comes. Actually, I care very little one way or another, it might be preferable if they did forget all about me.

For my part, I do not forget how inspired I am whenever I give my memory of certain Belgians free rein. That is the positive side, and the rest is of no more than secondary importance.

And here we are already in September, soon we'll be in the middle of autumn, and then winter.

I shall continue to work without let-up, and then if I have another attack around Christmas, we'll see, and when that's over, I can't see any objection to my telling the administration here to go to hell, and to my returning north for a fairly long time. To leave now, when I believe I may well have another attack this winter, that's to say in three months' time, would perhaps be too foolhardy.

It's been 6 weeks since I put a foot outdoors, even in the garden. Next week, however, when I've finished the canvases I'm busy with, I'm going to have a go.

But another few months and I'll be so flabby and lethargic that a change will probably do me a lot of good.

That's the way I'm thinking at the moment, though of course nothing is settled.

But I do believe that one shouldn't stand on ceremony with the people of this establishment, any more than with the proprietors of a hotel. We have rented a room from them for a certain length of time, and they are well paid for what they provide, and that's absolutely all there is to it.

Not to mention that they might like nothing better than for my condition to be chronic, and we would be unforgivably stupid to give in to them. They make far too many inquiries, to my mind, not only about what I, but also what you earn, &c.

So let's not quarrel with them and simply give them the slip.

I am continuing this letter again at intervals. Yesterday I began the portrait of the chief attendant, and I may do his wife as well, since he's married and lives in a little farmhouse a stone's throw from the institution.

A most interesting face. There's a beautiful etching by Legros of an old Spanish nobleman – if you remember it, it will give you an idea of the type. He was at the hospital in Marseilles during 2 cholera epidemics, in short, he is a man who has seen an enormous amount of death and suffering, and he has an indefinable expression of quiet contemplation, so that I am irresistibly reminded of Guizot's face – for there is something of that in this head, if different. But he is a man of the people and simpler. Anyway, you will see it if I succeed in doing it and if I make a copy of it.

I am struggling with all my might to keep my work under control by telling myself that success would be the best lightning conductor for my illness. I make sure I don't overdo things, and take care to keep myself to myself. It's selfish, if you like, not getting used to my companions in misfortune here and not going round to see them, but still, I feel none the worse for it, for my work is making headway, and that's what we need, for it is absolutely vital that I do better than before, as that was not enough.

Supposing I get out of here one day, wouldn't it be far better if I came back definitely capable of doing a portrait with some character than if I came back as I started? That's clumsily put, for I'm well aware one cannot say, 'I know how to do a portrait,' without telling a lie, because that is an infinite objective. Still you will understand what I mean, that I must do better than before.

At the moment my mind is working in an orderly way, and I feel completely normal – and when I look at my present condition, in the hope of generally having, between the attacks – if, unfortunately, it has to be expected that they will return from time to time – of having in between times, periods of lucidity and of working – when I look at my present condition, then I do indeed tell myself that it won't do to become obsessed with being sick. And that I must steadfastly continue my humble career as a painter. And so, staying for good in an asylum would probably be going too far.

A few days ago, I was reading in the Figaro about a Russian writer who also suffered from a nervous illness of which, moreover, he sadly died, and which brought on terrible attacks from time to time. But what is one to do? There is no remedy, or if there is one, it is to work with a will.

I am dwelling on this longer than I should.

All in all, I <u>prefer</u> to be definitely ill like this than to be the way I was in Paris when all this was coming on.

You will also see that when you put the portrait with the light background that I've just done next to those portraits I did of myself in Paris, you really will see that I look saner now than I did then, indeed much more so.

I am even inclined to believe that the portrait will tell you better than my letter how I am, and that it will reassure you – it took me a lot of trouble.

And the reaper is also going well, I think – it is very, very simple.

By the end of the month I'd go so far as to say you can count on 12 size 30 canvases, but in most cases they will be the same picture twice over, a study and the final painting.

Still, perhaps my journey to the south will yet bear fruit, for the stronger light and the blue sky teaches you to see, especially, or even only, if you see it all for a long time.

The north will undoubtedly seem quite new to me, and I have looked at things so much here that I have become very attached to them, so I shall feel sad for a long time.

Something odd occurs to me – in Manette Salomon there is a discussion of modern art, and some artist or other, talking of 'what will last', says that what will last is 'the landscape painters' – that view has already been proved true to some extent, for Corot, Daubigny, Dupré, Rousseau and Millet do endure as landscape painters, and when Corot said on his deathbed, 'I saw landscapes in a dream with skies all pink, it was charming,' well, yes, we see those skies all pink in Monet, Pissarro and Renoir, so the landscape painters do last very well, it's quite true. We'll leave aside the figure painting of Delacroix and Millet.

In any case, what is it that we are now beginning hesitantly to recognize as original and long-lasting? <u>Portraiture</u>. You might say that it's old stuff, but it's also quite new. We'll talk about it again – but we must never stop being on the lookout for portraits, especially by such artists as Guillaumin – that portrait of the young girl by Guillaumin! – and take good care of my portrait by Russell which I'm so fond of. Have you framed Laval's portrait? I don't think you told me what you thought of it. I thought it splendid, that gaze through the glasses, such a frank gaze.

My urge to do portraits is very strong these days, in fact Gauguin and I talked about this and similar matters until our nerves were strained to the point of stifling all human warmth.

But I dare say some good pictures will come out of it, and that's what we're after. And I should imagine they'll be doing some good work in Brittany. I got a letter from G., I think I already told you, and one day I should very much like to see what they are doing.

I must ask you for the following painting requisites.

> 10 metres of canvas
> Large tubes 6 tubes zinc white
>   "   "   2   "   emerald green
>   "   "   2   "   cobalt

<u>small</u> tubes

2 carmine
1 vermilion
1 large tube ordinary lake
6 Sable brushes, black hair

Then I promised the attendant here a copy of Le Monde illustré, No. 1684, 6 July 1889, in which there is a very pretty engraving after Demont-Breton.

Aha! The reaper is finished. I think it'll be one of those you'll keep at home – it's an image of death as the great book of nature speaks of it – but the effect I've been looking for is – 'on the point of smiling'. It's all yellow, except for a line of purple hills. A pale and golden yellow. I find it odd that I saw it like that through the iron bars of a cell.

Well, do you know what I hope for, once I allow myself to begin to hope? It is that the family will be for you what nature, the clods of earth, the grass, the yellow wheat, the peasant, are for me, in other words, that you find in your love for people something <u>not only to work for</u>, but to comfort and restore you when there is a need. So, I beg you not to let yourself get too exhausted by business, but to take good care of yourselves, both of you – perhaps there will still be some good in the not too distant future.

I've a good mind to do the reaper over again for Mother. If not, I'll do another picture for her birthday – it will be coming later, as I'll send it on with the rest.

For I'm convinced Mother would understand it – since

it is, in fact, as simple as one of those primitive woodcuts one finds in farmers' almanacs.

Send me the canvas as soon as you can, for if I still want to do other copies for the sisters, and if I am to make a start on the new autumn effects, I'll have enough to fill my time from the beginning of this month to the end.

I'm eating and drinking like a horse at present. I must say the doctor is taking very good care of me.

Yes, I do think that it's a good idea to do some pictures for Holland, for Mother and our two sisters. That will make three, that's to say the <u>Reaper, the Bedroom, the Olive Trees, Wheat Field and Cypress</u>. It will even make four, for there's somebody else I'm going to do one for as well.

I shall work at that, of course, with as much pleasure as for the Vingtistes, and more calmly. Since I feel strong, you may be sure that I shall get through a lot of work.

I am choosing the best from the 12 subjects, so that what they'll get will have been thought about a bit and specially picked. And then, it's a good thing to work for people who don't know what a picture is.

A good handshake for you and Jo,

Vincent

625 [F]

[2 February 1890]

My dear Theo,

I have just received your good news that you are a father at last, that Jo is over the most critical period, and finally that the little boy is doing well. That has done me more good and given me more pleasure than I can put into words. Bravo – and how pleased Mother will be! The day before yesterday I received a fairly long, very calm letter from her as well. So what I have been longing for so much and for such a long time has happened at last. No need to tell you that my thoughts have often turned to you of late, and it touched me very much that Jo had the kindness to write to me only the night before. How brave and calm she was at her moment of peril, it touched me very much. Well, it all helps a great deal in making me forget these last days when I was ill – at such times I no longer know where I am and my mind wanders.

I was extremely surprised by the article on my paintings you sent me. No need to tell you that I hope to keep thinking that I don't paint like that, but I do gather from it how I ought to be painting. For the article is absolutely right in the way it shows the gap to be filled, and I think that the writer really wrote it to guide, not only me, but all the other impressionists, and even to help them make the breach in the right place. So he proposes an ideal collective ego to the others quite as much as to me. He simply tells me that here and there he can see something good, if you like, even in my work which is so imperfect, and that is the comforting part, which I appreciate and for which I hope I am grateful. Only it ought to be understood that my back is not broad enough to be saddled with that task, and I need not tell you that, in concentrating the article on me, he has made me feel steeped in flattery. In my opinion it is all as exaggerated as a certain article by Isaäcson about you which claimed that present-day artists had given up quarrelling, and that an important movement was silently taking shape in the little shop on the Boulevard Montmartre. I admit that it is difficult to say what one means, to express oneself properly – just as one cannot paint things as one sees them – and so this isn't really a criticism of Isaäcson's <u>rashness</u>, or that of the other critic, but as far as we are concerned, well, we are merely serving as <u>model</u>, and that is surely a duty and a task like any other. So, should you or I acquire some sort of reputation, then we must simply try to take it as calmly as possible, and to keep our heads.

Why not say what he said of my sunflowers, and <u>with far greater justification</u>, of those magnificent and quite perfect hollyhocks of Quost's and his yellow irises, and those splendid peonies of Jeannin's? You know as well as I do that there is <u>always</u> another side of the coin to such praise. But I am glad, and very grateful for the article, or rather 'la coeur à l'aise',* as the revue song has it, since

---

* Glad at heart

one may need it, as one may indeed have need of a coin. Moreover, an article like that has its own merit as a critical work of art. As such I think it is to be respected and the writer must raise the tone, harness his conclusions, &c.

But from the outset, you should guard against allowing your young family <u>too much</u> contact with the artistic world. Old Goupil guided his household well through the Parisian undergrowth, and I imagine you still think of him often. Things have changed so much, today. His cold aloofness would meet resistance today, yet his capacity to weather so many storms was something special.

Gauguin proposed, very vaguely it is true, that we found a studio in his name, he, De Haan and I, but he insisted on seeing his Tonkin project through first. He seems to have cooled off a great deal, I'm not sure exactly why, about continuing to paint. And he is just the kind of man to clear off to Tonkin, in fact he needs some room to expand, and finds the life of an artist – and there is some truth in this – a mean one.

With all his experience of travel, what is one to say to him?

So I hope that he will feel that you and I are indeed his friends, without counting on us too much, which, it must be added, he in no way does. He writes with a great deal of reserve, and more seriously than last year. I have just sent another note to Russell to jog his memory about Gauguin, for I know that Russell is very reliable and a sound character. And should I get back together with Gauguin, then we would have need of Russell. Gauguin and Russell are countrymen at heart – not uncivilized, but with the innate mellow-ness of distant fields, probably much more than you or I – that is how they look to me.

True enough, one must sometimes have a little faith to see that. If I, for my part, wanted to go on with, let us call it the <u>translation</u> of certain pages of Millet, then to prevent people – not from criticizing me, that would be all right – but from hampering or stopping me by making out that all I do is produce copies – then – I need the support of people like Russell or Gauguin from among the artists to carry my project through and to make a serious job of it. I have scruples of con-science about doing the things by Millet you sent me, for example, and which seemed to me perfectly chosen, and so I took the pile of photographs and sent them straight to Russell, lest I see them again before I have thought it over. I don't want to do it before having heard something of what you and certain others think of the things you will soon be receiving.

Else I should be having scruples of conscience, fearing that it might be plagiarism. And not now, but in a few months' time, I shall try to obtain the frank opinion of Russell himself on the real usefulness of the thing. In any case, Russell is on a short fuse, he gets angry, and says what's what, and that is what I sometimes need. You know that I find the Virgin so dazzling that <u>I haven't dared</u> look at it. I felt an immediate 'not yet'. My illness makes me very sensitive right now, and I don't feel cap-able for the moment of continuing these 'translations' when such masterpieces are involved. I am stopping with the Sower on which I am working, and which is not coming on as I would wish. Being ill, however, I have thought a great deal about going on with the work. <u>When I do it, I do it calmly</u>, as you will soon see when I send you the five or 6 finished canvases.

I hope that M. Lauzet will come, I very much wish to make his acquaintance. I trust his opinion and when he says it [my painting] is Provence, he begs the question, and like the other critic he talks more about something yet to be done than about something already accomplished. Landscapes with cypresses! Ah, that wouldn't be easy – Aurier is aware of that, too, when he says that even black is a colour, and refers to their flaming appearance. I am thinking about it, but dare do nothing more, and like the cautious Isaäcson, I say that I don't think we are there yet. One needs a dose of inspiration, a ray from on high that is not in ourselves, to do beautiful things. When I had done those Sunflowers, I looked for the opposite and yet the equivalent, and said – it's the cypress.

I'm going to stop here – I am a little anxious about a friend who, it seems, is still ill, and whom I should like to see. She is the one whose portrait I did in yellow and black, and she has changed very much. She has nervous attacks, complicated by a premature change of life, in short, very painful. She looked like an old grandfather the last time. I had promised to come back in a fortnight, but was taken ill again myself.

Anyhow, as far as I'm concerned, the good news you've given me, and that article, and a whole lot of things have made me feel quite well today. I'm sorry that M. Salles did not find you. I want to thank Wil once again for her kind letter. I should have liked to have replied to it today, but am putting it off for a few days. Tell her that Mother has written me another long letter from Amsterdam. How happy she will be, Wil too!

I am with you all in my thoughts, though ending my letter. May Jo long remain for us what she is now. As for the little boy, why don't you name him Theo, in memory of our Father, that would certainly give me much pleasure.

A handshake,

Ever yours,
Vincent

In the meantime, if you see him, thank M. Aurier very much for his article. I shall of course be sending you a note for him, and a study.

626A [F] [LETTER FROM VINCENT TO ALBERT AURIER]

[10 or 11 February 1890]

Dear M. Aurier,

Thank you very much for your article in the <u>Mercure de France</u>, which surprised me a good deal. I admire it very much as a work of art in itself, it seems to me that you paint with words; in fact, I encounter my canvases anew in your article, but better than they are in reality, richer, more meaningful. Reflecting, however, that what you say would be more relevant to others than to myself, I feel uneasy. Monticelli in particular is a case in point. Since you say that 'he is, so far as I know, the only painter who perceives the range of colour of things with this intensity, with this metallic, gem-like quality', please go to see, at my brother's, a certain bouquet by Monticelli – a bouquet in white, forget-me-not blue & orange – and then you will understand what I mean. But for some time now the best, the most wonderful Monticellis have been in Scotland and England. There should still be a marvellous one of his in a gallery in the North – the one in Lille, I think – as rich and certainly no less French than Le départ pour Cythère by Watteau. At this moment M. Lauzet is in the process of reproducing about thirty Monticellis. As far as I know, there is no colourist who stems so directly from Delacroix, and yet it is probable, in my opinion, that Monticelli knew of Delacroix's colour theories at second-hand only; he had them in particular from Diaz and Ziem. Monticelli's artistic temperament seems to me exactly the same as that of the author of the Decameron – Boccaccio – a melancholy, rather resigned, unhappy man, watching the fashionable wedding party and the lovers of his time pass him by, painting them and analysing them – he, the outsider. Oh! He no more imitated Boccaccio than Henri Leys imitated the primitives.

Anyway – what I am trying to say is that things seem

to have mistakenly become attached to my name that you would do better to link to Monticelli, to whom I owe so much. I also owe a great deal to Paul Gauguin, with whom I worked for several months in Arles, and whom, moreover, I already knew in Paris.

Gauguin, that curious artist, that strange individual, whose demeanour and look vaguely recall Rembrandt's Portrait of a Man at the Galerie Lacaze – that friend who likes to make one feel that a good picture should be equivalent to a good deed, not that he says so, but it is in fact difficult to be much in his company without being mindful of a certain moral responsibility. A few days before we parted company, when my illness forced me to go into an asylum, I tried to paint 'his empty place'.

It is a study of his wooden armchair, brown and dark red, the seat of greenish straw, and in place of the absent person, a lighted candle in a candlestick and some modern novels. Should the opportunity arise, do please take another look at this study by way of a reminder of him. It is done throughout in broken tones of green and red.

You may realize now that your article would have been fairer and – it seems to me – consequently more powerful, if, when dealing with the question of the future of 'tropical painting' and the question of colour, you had – before speaking of me – done justice to Gauguin and Monticelli. <u>For the role attaching to me, or that will be attached to me, will remain, I assure you, of very secondary importance</u>.

Besides, I should like to ask you another question. Let us suppose that the two canvases of sunflowers which are at present at the Vingtistes have certain qualities of colour, and that they also symbolize 'gratitude'. Are they any different from so many other pictures of flowers, more skilfully painted, which are not yet appreciated enough – the Roses trémières and the Iris jaunes by old Quost, the magnificent bunches of peonies which Jeannin produces in such abundance? You see, I find it very difficult to make a distinction between impressionism and other things. I do not see any use for much of the sectarian thinking we have seen these last few years, <u>but the absurdity of it frightens me</u>.

And in conclusion, I confess I do not understand why you should vilify Meissonier. It may have been from the excellent Mauve that I have inherited a boundless admiration for Meissonier; Mauve was tireless in his praise of Troyon and Meissonier – a strange combination.

I say this in order to draw your attention to how much people from other countries admire the artists of France without attaching the slightest importance to what, unfortunately, so often divides them. An often-repeated saying of Mauve's was something like, 'If one wants to use colour, one should also be able to draw an inglenook or an interior like Meissonier.'

If you will do me the pleasure of accepting it, I shall include a study of cypresses for you in the next batch I send to my brother, in remembrance of your article. I am still working on it at the moment, as I want to put a small figure into it. The cypress is so characteristic of the Provence landscape. You will feel it, and say, 'Even the colour black.' Until now, I have not been able to do them as I feel them; the emotions that come over me in the face of nature can be so intense that I lose consciousness, and the result is a fortnight during which I cannot do any work. However, before leaving here, I mean to have one more try at tackling the cypresses. The study I intend for you represents a group of them in the corner of a wheat field during the mistral on a summer's day. It is thus a kind of black note in the shifting blue of the flowing wide sky, with the vermilion of the poppies contrasting with the note of black. You will see that it forms something like the combination of tones found in those agreeable Scottish tartans of green, blue, red, yellow and black, which seemed so charming to you and to me at the time, and which, alas, we hardly see any more these days.

In the meantime, dear Sir, please accept my grateful thanks for your article. If I come to Paris in the spring, I certainly shall not fail to thank you in person.

Vincent v. Gogh

Auvers-sur-Oise

W22 [F] [letter from Vincent to Wil]

[3 June 1890]

My dear sister,

I should have replied long ago to your two letters, which I received while still at St Rémy, but the journey, the work, and a great many new emotions made me put off writing from one day to the next until now. I was very interested to learn that you had been nursing patients at the Walloon hospital. That is certainly the way to learn a great deal, the best & the most useful things one can learn, and I for one regret that I know nothing, or at any rate not enough, about it all.

It gave me great joy to see Theo again, and to make the acquaintance of Jo and the little one. Theo's cough was worse than when I last saw him more than 2 years ago, but in talking to him and seeing him close at hand, I certainly found him, all things considered, changed somewhat for the better, and Jo is full of good sense and good will. The little one isn't sickly, but he isn't strong either. If one lives in a big city, it is a good system for the wife to go to the country for her confinement and to stay there with the baby for the first few months. But seeing that the first confinement is especially difficult they certainly could not have done better or otherwise than they did. I am hoping that they will come here to Auvers soon for a few days.

As for me, the journey & everything else have gone well so far, and coming back north has taken my mind off things a great deal. And then I have found a perfect friend in Dr Gachet, something like another brother – so alike are we physically, and mentally, too. He is very nervous and most odd himself and has been a great friend & help, so far as he was able, to the artists of the new school. I did his portrait the other day and am also going to do one of his daughter, who is 19 years old. He lost his wife some years ago, which was the main reason for his being laid low. We became instant friends, so to speak, and I shall go and stay with him one or two days every week to work in his garden, of which I have already painted two studies, one with plants of the south, aloes, cypresses, marigolds, and the other with some white roses, a vine and a figure, and then a clump of ranunculus. As well as that, I've done a larger picture of the village church – with an effect in which the building appears purplish-blue against a sky of deep & simple blue, pure cobalt. The stained-glass windows appear as patches of ultramarine, the roof is purple and partly orange. In the foreground a little greenery in bloom and some pink sunlit sand. Again, it's very similar to the studies I did in Nuenen of the old tower and the churchyard. Only now the colour is probably more expressive, more sumptuous. But towards the end at St Rémy I was still working like one possessed, especially on bunches of flowers, roses and purple irises.

I brought back quite a large picture for Theo and Jo's little one – which they have hung above the piano – white almond blossom – large branches against a sky-blue background, and they've also got a new portrait of the Arlésienne in their apartment. My friend Dr Gachet is <u>decidedly enthusiastic</u> about this last portrait of the Arlésienne, of which I have also kept a copy for myself, and about a self-portrait, and I was pleased about that, as he's persuading me to do some figure painting and will be finding me some interesting models to do, I hope. What fascinates me much, much more than it does all the others in my trade – is the portrait, the modern portrait. I am attempting it with colour, and am certainly not alone in attempting it this way. I <u>should like</u> – you see, I'm far from saying that I can, but I'm going to try anyway – I <u>should like</u> to do portraits which will appear as revelations to people in a hundred years' time. In other words, I am not trying to achieve this by photographic likeness but by rendering our impassioned expressions, by using our modern knowledge and appreciation of colour as a means of rendering and exalting character. So the portrait of Dr Gachet shows you a face the colour of an over-heated brick, burnt by the sun, with red hair and a white cap, against a landscape with a background of blue hills. His clothes are ultramarine, which brings out his face and makes it look pale even though it is brick-coloured. His hands, the hands of an obstetrician, are paler than his face. In front of him on a red garden table are yellow novels and a dark red foxglove flower. My self-portrait is done in almost the same way, but the blue is a delicate southern blue, and the clothes are pale lilac. The portrait of the Arlésienne has a colourless and matt flesh tone, the eyes are calm and very simple, the clothing is black, the background pink, and she is leaning on a green table with green books. But in the copy that Theo has, the clothing is pink, the background yellowy-white, and the front of the open bodice is muslin in a white that merges into green. Among all these light colours, only the hair, the eyelashes and the eyes form black patches.

I'm not managing to do a very good sketch of it.

There is a superb picture by Puvis de Chavannes at the exhibition. The figures are dressed in bright colours, and one cannot tell if they are present-day costumes or clothes from olden times. On one side two women in simple long gowns are talking, on the other side men who look like artists, and in the centre a woman with a child in her arms is picking a flower from an apple tree in blossom. One figure is forget-me-not blue, another bright lemon yellow, another soft pink, another white, another violet. They are shown on a meadow dotted with little white and yellow flowers. The far distance is blue, with a white town and a river. All humanity, all nature simplified, as they might be, if they are not already so.

This description tells you nothing, but on seeing the picture, and looking at it for a long time, you might think you are present at a renaissance, inevitable but benevolent, of all things in which one has believed, which one has longed for, a strange and happy meeting of far distant antiquities with crude modernity.

I was also pleased to see André Bonger again, who appeared strong and calm, and argued, upon my word, with much soundness about art.

I was delighted that he came while I was in Paris.

Thank you again for your letters, goodbye for now, I embrace you in thought,

Ever yours,
Vincent

649 [F]

[c. 10 July 1890]

Dear brother and sister,

The letter from Jo has really been like a gospel for me, a deliverance from the distress caused by the hours I shared with you, which were rather difficult & trying for us all. It is no small matter when we are all made aware that our daily bread is at risk, no small matter when for different reasons we are also made aware of the precariousness of our existence.

Back here, I, too, still felt very sad, and the storm which threatens you continued to weigh heavily on me as well. What is there to be done? Look, I try to be reasonably good-humoured in general, but my life is also under attack at its very root, my step is also unsteady.

I was afraid – not entirely – but a little nevertheless – that my being a burden to you was something you found intolerable – but Jo's letter proves to me clearly that you do realize that I am working and making an effort just as much as you are.

So – having arrived back here, I have set to work again – although the brush is nearly falling from my hands – and because I knew exactly what I wanted to do, I have painted three more large canvases. They are vast stretches of wheat under troubled skies, and I didn't have to put myself out very much in order to try and express sadness and extreme loneliness. I hope you'll be seeing them shortly since I'd like to bring them to you in Paris as soon as possible. I'm fairly sure these canvases will tell you what I cannot say in words, that is, how healthy and invigorating I find the countryside.

The third canvas is Daubigny's garden, a picture I've had in mind ever since I came here.

I hope with all my heart that the proposed journey will help a little to take your minds off things.

I often think of the little one, I don't doubt it's better to bring up children than to spend all one's nervous energy on making pictures, but it can't be helped, I am, or at least I feel I am, too old now to retrace my steps or to long for anything else. That longing has left me, but the mental suffering remains.

I was very sorry not to have seen Guillaumin again, but am pleased he's looked at my canvases. If I had waited for him, I should probably have stayed talking to him so long I would have missed my train.

Wishing you both luck, a stout heart and comparative prosperity, may I ask you to tell Mother and our sister once again that I think of them very often. Indeed, I had a letter from them this morning and will be replying soon.

Handshakes in thought,

Ever yours,
Vincent

My money won't last me very long this time, for on my return I had to pay the bill for the luggage from Arles. I have some very good memories of that journey to Paris. A few months ago I hardly dared hoped to see my friends again. I think that Dutch lady is most talented. Lautrec's picture, Portrait de musicienne, is quite wonderful, it moved me when I saw it.

651 [F]

[24 July 1890]

My dear brother,

Thank you for your letter of today and the enclosed 50 fr. note.

I should try, perhaps, to write to you about a great many things, but in the first place I have completely lost the inclination, and then, it seems useless to me.

I hope you found those gentlemen favourably disposed towards you.

As far as the peace of your household is concerned,

I am as much convinced that it can be preserved as I am that it is threatened by storms.

I would rather not forget the little French I know, and am certainly unable to see the sense in delving deeper into the rights or wrongs of one side or the other in any discussions. It wouldn't be my concern anyway.

Things move quickly here. Aren't Dries, you and I rather more convinced of that, don't we understand that rather better than those ladies? So much the better for them – but in the long run we can't even count on talking coolly about it.

As far as I am concerned, I am giving my canvases my undivided attention. I am trying to do as well as some painters I have greatly loved and admired.

Now I have returned, my feeling is that the painters themselves are increasingly at bay these days.

All right . . . but hasn't the moment for trying to make them understand the usefulness of an association already passed? On the other hand an association, should it come about, would go under if the rest were to go under. In that case, you might say, the dealers could throw their lot in with the impressionists – but that would be very short-lived. All in all, it seems to me that personal initiative is of no avail, and, given the experience we've had, should we really be starting all over again?

I've noted with pleasure that the Gauguin from Brittany I saw is very beautiful, and it seems to me that the others he's done there will probably be so as well.

Perhaps you'll take a look at this sketch of Daubigny's garden – it is one of my most carefully thought-out canvases. I am adding a sketch of old thatched roofs and sketches of two size 30 canvases representing vast stretches of wheat after the rain. Hirschig has asked if you would be kind enough to order him the enclosed list of paints from the same dealer where you buy my paints.

Tasset could send them to him direct, cash on delivery, but then he'd have to give him the 20% discount, which would be the simplest. Or else you could put them in the batch of paints for me, adding the bill, or telling me how much the total amount comes to, and then he would send the money to you. You can't get good paints here. I have cut my own order to the absolute minimum.

Hirschig is beginning to get a better idea of things, it seems to me. He has done a portrait of the old schoolmaster, who has given him a 'well done'. And then he has some landscape studies which are almost the same colour as the Konings at your place. They may turn out to be just like these, or like the things by Voerman we saw together.

Goodbye for now, keep well and good luck in business, etc., remember me to Jo and handshakes in thought,

Ever yours,
Vincent

Van Gogh died in his brother's arms five days after writing this letter, from injuries caused by a self-inflicted gunshot wound.